Case Studies in the Ethics of Assisted Reproduction

Louise P. King • Isabelle C. Band

Editors

Case Studies in the Ethics of Assisted Reproduction

 Springer

Editors
Louise P. King
Center for Bioethics
Harvard Medical School
Boston, MA, USA

Isabelle C. Band
Icahn School of Medicine at Mount Sinai
New York, NY, USA

ISBN 978-3-031-41214-1   ISBN 978-3-031-41215-8   (eBook)
https://doi.org/10.1007/978-3-031-41215-8

This Springer imprint is published by the registered company Springer Nature Switzerland AG
The registered company address is: Gewerbestrasse 11, 6330 Cham, Switzerland

Paper in this product is recyclable.

Foreword

Nowhere in Medicine is the need in ethical guidance more indispensable than in the field of Assisted Reproduction. Negotiating assisted reproductive technologies (ART) such as in vitro fertilization (IVF), let alone permutations thereof, requires an altogether new world view. Scarcely 45 year in the making, Assisted Reproduction is all about the possible which was all but impossible a mere semicentennial ago. The vortex wherein ART and morality collide is hurtling forward ever faster along blind curves that were all but unforeseen. Who in their right mind could have imagined the advent of in vitro-derived gametes, of same sex reproduction, or of germline editing as recently as a decade ago? It is here that lifeguards in the form of *Case Studies in the Ethics of Assisted Reproduction* step in to lend a hand. Absent such, little can be done to preclude the proverbial drowning of ART practitioners in what remains an ever-novel medical enterprise. It follows that mastering the missives delivered by *Case Studies in the Ethics of Assisted Reproduction* should be the goal of all new entrants into the ART field. Then, and only then, can one lay claim to a discipline whose goal it is to address the plight of those whose shattered reproductive hopes are in need of shoring up.

Natural reproduction, the essence of humanity, remains work in progress. The story of Adam and Eve is still being revised with no obvious conclusion in sight. Assisted Reproduction, the latest wrinkle in this ever-evolving saga, is neither self-evident nor self-explanatory. This is precisely why *Case Studies in the Ethics of Assisted Reproduction* is indispensable. What this all-important compilation of essays strives to achieve is to fill in the blanks. The serious practice of Assisted Reproduction demands nothing less. This all-important goal is being subserved herein by an impressive compilation of legal scholars, bioethicists, reproductive endocrinologists, and reproductive biologists. It does not get much better than this. It is for these reasons that a significant debt of gratitude is due Louise P. King, MD, JD (Assistant Professor of Obstetrics, Gynecology and Reproductive Biology, Harvard Medical School) and Isabelle Band, BA, whose tireless efforts have made *Case Studies in the Ethics of Assisted Reproduction* a reality.

Warren Alpert Medical School, Brown University   Eli Y. Adashi
Providence, RI, USA

Preface and Acknowledgments

The casebook that follows was developed over years with the collaboration of a variety of contributors. It was conceived as a resource for a wide audience.

We have gathered experts from ethics, law, and medicine to discuss typical clinical scenarios that arise in assisted reproduction accompanied by ethical analysis.

Our goal is to create a starting point for discussion of these topics at the undergraduate, graduate, masters, and doctoral level. It is not an exhaustive exploration of the topics presented but instead a resource from which to delve into further reading and exploration.

The book includes a primer on reproductive bioethics and legal considerations in assisted reproduction. If a single case is chosen to be discussed in any particular class or setting, we strongly encourage inclusion of those introductory chapters in the assignment.

Each case is followed by a discussion of medical principles at play and then a summary of ethical considerations as well as the typical resolution in clinical practice. This is not meant to indicate that this is the perfect or "right" solution. Instead, it reflects one approach.

We would like to note that the chapters, which were written by independent authors, utilize different terms to refer to pregnancy-capable individuals. Some chapters use "pregnant woman," while others use non-gendered terms such as "pregnant person." We acknowledge that any individual with a uterus, regardless of gender identity or expression, may be capable of becoming pregnant. Gendered language such as "pregnant woman" may also be more accurate in certain chapters where the case specifies that the patient is a cisgender woman.

Finally, we wish to acknowledge the essential contributions of the following in no particular order: Alan S. Penzias, MD; Edward M. Hundert, MD; Katherine L. Watson, JD; Christine Mitchell, RN, MS, MTS, HEC-C; Robert D. Truog, MD, MA; Rebecca Weintraub Brendel, MD, JD; Anthony C. Breu, MD; Vardit Ravitsky, PhD; Jonathan Marron, MD, MPH.

Boston, MA, USA   Louise P. King

New York, NY, USA   Isabelle C. Band

Contents

Part I
Introduction to Fertility Medicine and Ethics

Basic Primer on Principles and Philosophy Applicable to Reproductive Bioethics

Natasha Aljalian and Louise P. King

Abstract Various principles and frameworks are useful in guiding ethical shared decision making as well as policy development in reproductive medicine. These include: ethical theories (e.g., principilism, utilitarianism) and principles (e.g., moral status) as well as additional considerations (e.g., informed consent). No one of these ethical models or frameworks must be adopted or should be applied unilaterally. In some cases, the application of varied ethical models may yield to conflicting outcomes. Nevertheless, each of these theories gives rise to considerations which are important to consider to completely appreciate the complex ethical dimensions of moral dilemmas in reproductive ethics. This chapter will serve as a reference point for all chapters that follow to provide background and context for ethical theories used elsewhere in this casebook.

Keywords Reproductive ethics · Principlism · Common morality · Utilitarianism · Moral status

Framework for Analysis

The first step when faced with a dilemma in reproductive medicine is to identify and specify the ethical question that must be resolved. In order to do this, one must gather and understand the relevant facts, information, and context in the case. This process includes carefully identifying all stakeholders to ensure varied, sometimes

N. Aljalian
Office of Technology Development, Harvard University, Cambridge, MA, USA

Office of Ethics, Boston Children's Hospital, Boston, MA, USA

L. P. King (✉)
Center for Bioethics, Harvard Medical School, Boston, MA, USA

© The Author(s), under exclusive license to Springer Nature
Switzerland AG 2023
L. P. King, I. C. Band (eds.), *Case Studies in the Ethics of Assisted Reproduction*, https://doi.org/10.1007/978-3-031-41215-8_1

overlapping interests are included in analysis. Additionally, it is important to define what medical decisions and considerations preclude various paths forward. Sometimes, the requested path is not medically possible in which case no ethical question need be resolved.

Finally, the team should synthesize this information and formulate the ethical question, which might be specified as:

- "Given [facts/conflicting values/disagreement/etc.], what decisions or actions are ethically justifiable?" or
- "Given [facts/conflicting values/disagreement/etc.], is it ethically justifiable to [do/not do act] [take/not take action]?"

The ethical analysis (utilizing principles and considerations set forth below) follows.

Ethical Theories

Here we summarize several ethical theories and principles. These are not proscriptive, and we do not propose that any one of these ethical models be adopted and applied *en toto*. It may be the case that application of the following ethical models may yield to different or conflicting outcomes. Nevertheless, each of these theories gives rise to considerations which are important to take into account in order to completely appreciate and consider the complex ethical dimensions of moral dilemmas in reproductive ethics.

Principlism and the Common Morality

British physician Thomas Percival "furnished the first developed modern account of healthcare ethics."[1] Beauchamp and Childress's "principlism" approach was a notable shift from Percival's beneficence-based health care ethics. Principlism provided a shift from previous paternalistic approaches, providing health care providers a set of principles which placed greater emphasis on autonomy and reflected concerns of social justice.

Principlism is a pluralistic ethical theory that is recognized, widely accepted, and commonly utilized in medical/biomedical ethics which calls upon general principles to assist in ethical reasoning. The approach acknowledges that monistic approaches (which find their grounding in one underlying theory or principle) are insufficient for the complex determinations to be made in medical ethics. By comparison, principlism – one type of pluralistic approach – is grounded in more than

---

[1] Beauchamp at 38 (referencing Percival).

one moral theory or principle, specifically, a "common morality," a universal social compact acknowledging that there are key, fundamental moral truths on which all moral people would agree.[2] A benefit of utilizing principles based in the notion of a "common morality" is that these principles can be easily understood and applied in the healthcare field and in other relevant, professional fields.[3] Principlism offers four equal principles thought to be accepted and shared by all individuals: autonomy, beneficence, nonmaleficence, and justice.[4]

- *Autonomy* – Autonomy is "a principle requiring respect for the decision-making capacities of autonomous persons." It imbues into moral analysis a respect for self-determination and human dignity; a respect for the voluntary intentional decisions made by those who are self-aware, or put differently, have decision-making capacity. Autonomy is a highly valued Western construct. It is a marked shift from the prevailing approach in other cultures and, according to some views, when overly emphasized, undermines the ability of healthcare providers to exercise professional, independent medical judgment.
- *Beneficence* – Beneficence is a positive obligation to "do good" and provide a benefit to patients. Beneficence towards patients is a commonly-accepted fundamental cornerstone of healthcare, described "as a foundational value - and sometimes as *the* foundational value – in health care ethics." The challenge is not whether beneficence has a role in healthcare, but defining and determining what is "good," is a patient's "welfare," minimizes harm or suffering, or the "best outcome for a patient."[5] Beyond the challenge of defining what is "best" for an individual patient is that these decisions have cumulative effects that extend far beyond one patient and specific, individual intended outcomes. They bear greater implications about what is "good" for the medical profession, for society, and for humanity (whether intended or unintended, foreseen and unforeseen).[6]
- *Nonmaleficence* – Nonmaleficence is a corollary to the concept of beneficence, and embodies the physician's maxim *primum non nocere* – "above all, do no harm." Percival maintained that "nonmaleficence comports with physician's primary and fiduciary obligations and 'fixes the physician's primary obligations and triumphs even over the principle of respect for the patient's autonomy in a circumstance of potential harm to patients.'"[7] Some extend this notion, asserting that physicians must not only "do no harm," but should refrain from acts which cause or facilitate harm.

---

[2] Beauchamp and Childress at 7.

[3] These principles are set forth in Beauchamp and Childress (99–313).

[4] These four principles originate from the Belmont Report, which sought to protect human research participants, and from foundational bioethics texts.

[5] King, *Autonomy*.

[6] *See* Jasanoff at 249, 256.

[7] Beauchamp and Childress at 162–164.

- *Justice* – There are many conceptions of justice - distributive, egalitarian, restorative, fairness- based. Ultimately, justice focuses on some fundamental considerations: analyzing equality and equity of basic rights and duties; a fair and appropriate distribution of benefits, risks, burdens, and costs; a value-based conception of the "right"; like individuals being treated equally; and individuals being treated according to what is "due, fair, and owed." Justice issues include access, due process, and the imposition of unjustifiable harms, unfounded judgments, or unfair placement of limitations or burdens on certain demographics or populations.[8]

Additional Ethical Theories and Principles

While principlism often forms the basis for moral reasoning and ethical decision making within modern health care ethics in the United States, there are other ethical theories (some of which have historically heavily influenced reproductive health and research) that are important to consider when engaging moral dilemmas in reproductive health.

Moral Status

An important threshold consideration when considering any reproductive issue is the moral status (referenced by some as moral value or moral worth) granted various individuals or entities, and our resulting moral treatment of or consideration for each. This determination is helpful, for example, in ensuring that we meet a central guiding principle of bioethics – treating like cases alike.

Utilitarianism

Utilitarianism is a monistic, consequentialist theory based on one underlying theory: desiring acts that maximize the overall benefit to, or good of, society. This approach focuses on the consequences or outcomes of an action. An inherent challenge (similar to beneficence) of this theory is defining what is "good" for or "benefits" society. Under "act utilitarianism," one focuses on the likelihood of an act benefiting society. A primary shortcoming of this approach is its subjective nature and the uncertainty and unpredictability of outcomes. "Rule utilitarianism"

---

[8] *See, e.g.,* Sandel, Goodwin.

approaches things slightly differently; acts are morally permissible if they adhere to a rule that leads to societal good, or the benefit of the most people. More objective than its counterpart, rule utilitarianism would assert that if "there is strong evidence to support the view that the use of reproductive technology will lead to a society in which the welfare of its members will not be served, then a rule utilitarian would be on firm ground in arguing that reproductive technology ought to be abandoned."[9]

Deontology

Also a monistic theory, Kant's ethical theory revolves around duty – duties to oneself and to others. Deontology places moral value on beings with the ability to reason; rational beings are viewed to have inherent dignity. This gives rise to other tenets. First, is the concept that humans must always act according to a rule, or maxim, that they would wish ("will") would be universalizable, or a "universal law of nature."[10] Next, is that humanity must never be treated as merely a means to an end, but as an end in itself. Deontology's focus on reason rather than emotions, intuition, or relationships, renders it – on its own – insufficient to employ in moral analysis. However, certain characteristics of deontology (for example, the focus on human autonomy and dignity, the role of reason, the importance of specific and general duties, and the claim that some acts are inherently wrong) are considerations that might play a role in ethical decision making.

W.D. Ross's Pluralism

Unlike utilitarianism and deontology, Ross's theory is a pluralistic approach akin to Beauchamp and Childress's principlism. Ross's pluralism holds that there is no one, controlling fundamental good or underlying moral principle or rule that determines the morality of an action. Ross would assert that actions may be "right" for one or more than one reason, and similarly wrong for one or more than one reason. Ross's pluralism claims there are a number of duties which help determine whether an action is "right" or "good."[11] This is based on what he defines as core duties, or prima facie obligations, of common-sense morality: a duty of *non-maleficence* (not to harm others); a duty of *fidelity* (to keep our promises); a duty of *reparation* (to rectify a previous wrong we have committed); a duty of *gratitude* (to return services to those from whom we have in the past accepted benefits); and a duty to *promote a*

---

[9] Munson at 383.

[10] Kant, *The Good Will and the Categorical Imperative.*

[11] Ross, *The Right and The Good,* at 21–27.

maximum of aggregate good.[12] Ross asserts that while there may be more than one moral duty to consider in a situation, in exercising moral judgment we must fulfill the duty that has the greatest weight to achieve the maximum aggregate good in a given situation, "all things considered."

Casuistry

Casuistry is an intermediate approach. While it employs principles, it goes beyond them. In casuistry, moral reasoning begins first by discerning morally relevant topics from the particulars of the case before the health care provider. Next, the analysis considers precedents and cases based on similar facts in similar circumstances. Finally, the provider engages in analogical reasoning to arrive at a moral judgment. While casuistry employs mid-level principles, it is different from principle-based approaches as it incorporates a "bottom up" approach from cases and case precedents, rather than a "top down" approach from theories or principles to specific cases. Casuistry is imperfect; it can be subjective and difficult to apply at times, and risks perpetuating improper moral conclusions. Nonetheless, it offers valuable insight and perspective when engaging in ethical analysis and forms the basis of this casebook.[13]

Ethics of Care/Feminine Ethics

It is important to consider corollaries or complements to monistic and pluralistic reason- and principle-based approaches. Ethics of care, or feminine ethics, broadens the approach to moral reasoning. It contemplates that perhaps women's cognitive approaches are not underdeveloped but instead are an entirely different way of thinking.[14] Ethics of care moves our consideration away from an ethics based on "rights" and "justice," and instead includes consideration of relationships, situatedness, and context in moral reasoning. It legitimizes the role of emotion, of caring for others, and of being invested in and responsible for others in moral decision making.[15]

---

[12] Ross, *The Right and The Good*, 21–27.

[13] *See* Jonsen.

[14] *See* Gilligan.

[15] *See* Gilligan.

Feminist Ethics

Feminist ethics is an approach to ethics which seeks to examine, and correct, the role of gender and gender-based values in our moral values and assessments. It seeks to analyze and remedy the historical and common privilege afforded to men, and the ways that gender norms and stereotypes promote and perpetuate "oppressive social orders or practices that harm others, especially girls and women who historically have been subordinated, along gendered dimensions including sexuality and gender-identity."[16] More specifically, it considers how individuals' identity and existence, marginalized social groups, and unjust systems and structures shape discourse. Feminist ethics has developed beyond gender to consider commonalities of the moral experiences of the marginalized and oppressed, and seeks to address and liberate individuals from the oppression that comes with belonging to any of the oppressed groups.[17] Moreover, it considers how intersectionality – an individual's identity and belonging to more than one oppressed group – both influences their experience but also exposes them to increased moral harm.

Narrative Ethics

Narrative ethics places great weight on individual cases, viewing each case as an individual narrative or story.[18] Some view narrative ethics as a standalone, non-principle-based theory, while others view it as a complementary method to the work of ethics. Whichever the position, narrative ethics provides – akin to casuistry - important perspective. It provides a lens through which to view moral theories and to test moral principles by applying them to specific cases. Rather than focusing on "where do we go from here?" the focus is on "how did we get here?" Factors considered by a narrative approach include: the characters in the narrative, including their consciousness, cognition, emotion, and views; understanding the chronology and timing of the case; the physical landscape, proximity to the situation, and pace of the case; and the role of gender, values, experience, and stereotypes. Like casuistry, it can lack objectivity; however, like feminist ethics it humanizes the context of moral reasoning, gives voice to the oppressed and marginalized, and can avoid the perpetuation of injustice.

---

[16] *See* Norlock.

[17] *See* Norlock, Scully.

[18] Chambers at 40.

Virtue Ethics

Virtue ethics differs in a material manner from the approaches set forth above. Its focus is on the individual at the center of the ethical dilemma. Virtue ethics focuses broadly on individuals' ongoing cultivation of a virtuous character. While it might be difficult to apply to a general population (e.g. asking what a "virtuous person would do" in a circumstance), it is intuitively appealing specifically in the health care environment, where within the code and aim of the profession, one can emulate a moral exemplar and ask: "What would the virtuous physician do?"

Reproductive Justice

Reproductive ethics is, most basically, a reference to ethical questions surrounding the beginning of life and human reproduction. As this textbook demonstrates, in actuality, Reproductive Ethics is one of the most complex and divisive areas of ethical thought. It is not theoretical or academic in nature; rather, it has real life impact. Reproductive Ethics is undeniably intertwined with other ethical, philosophical, theological, social, and legal approaches. Myriad questions arise in reproductive ethics, the most basic of which is whether reproduction is a fundamental human right. Emanating from this are countless other questions and considerations, for example, questions of moral status, bodily autonomy, conscientious objection, surrogacy, parental rights, termination of pregnancy, procreative beneficence and eugenics, equity and access to reproductive care, professional and parental duties and obligations, and the moral appropriateness of using certain assisted reproductive technologies to achieve reproduction.[19]

A germane yet standalone framework for consideration in ethical analysis, not to be confused with reproductive ethics, is Reproductive Justice. To summarize and properly discuss the important work of Reproductive Justice would take a chapter, or even an entire book, in itself. Sister Song, a non-profit reproductive justice collective, defines Reproductive Justice as "the human right to maintain personal bodily autonomy, have children, not have children, and parent the children we have in safe and sustainable communities."[20] This Reproductive Justice framework – which some might characterize more properly as a grassroots, human rights movement – is committed to justice, access, equity, and autonomy for all women, including and most notably women of color, disadvantaged, marginalized, and low-income women, and trans people. Reproductive Justice calls, among other things, for social, economic, and policy reform to ensure equitable access to education, contraception, reproductive care, decision-making, and opportunities.[21]

---

[19] *See* The Oxford Handbook of Reproductive Ethics. Oxford University Press. January 2016.
[20] *See* Sister Song.
[21] *See* In Our Own Voice, Sister Song.

Additional Considerations

Beyond the theory, principle-based and other approaches to moral reasoning, there are additional concepts and considerations to be considered and appreciated in the work of bioethics. While some of these are often rooted in ethical principles such as respect for autonomy or beneficence, they are important to bear in mind as stand-alone considerations.

For example:

- Beyond its importance in the legal context, *informed consent* is a crucial safeguard. This is primarily due to its importance in respecting a patient's autonomy and personal values and avoiding paternalistic decisions of what health care providers think is best for the patient in a given situation. True informed consent respects a person's dignity, enables an individual's self-determination, allows patients to make decisions for themselves, helps the patient avoid or knowingly assume known harms, protects against abusive actions, and, importantly, focuses on the importance of trust in the relationship.[22] It informs the patient about levels of invasiveness (physical and psychological), complexity, alternatives, reversibility, as well as known (and the risk of potentially unknown) risks.
- *Avoiding conflicts of interest* is important; in other words, avoiding the risk that the primary interest of patient health is not unduly influenced by secondary interest such as "seeking one's own prestige or professional or financial interests, or pleasing patients."[23] Conflicts frequently exist. Identifying these conflicts and resolving them in favor of the interests of the patient is an ethical response.
- The *role that religion and faith communities and various cultures* continue to play in reproductive medicine. These faith and cultural values are deeply held, personal beliefs. It is helpful to understand their views so as to engage patients in discourse on patient care and decision making.
- *Cultural relativism* is a form of moral relativism which would hold that an act is right or wrong, or good or bad, depending on the moral code – or the system of rules or norms - of the culture in which one belongs.[24] One challenge is that diverse cultural codes may conflict, for example because cultures disagree on the respective moral norms.[25] While one should consider, be sensitive to, and respect patient's cultural norms[26]; the challenge is determining how best to proceed when a patient's cultural norms conflict with the culture in which reproductive care is being provided.

---

[22] *See* O'Neill, *Some Limits of Informed Consent. See also* O'Neill, Autonomy, and Luna and Luker.
[23] *See* Emmanuel.
[24] Sandel at 42. Timmons at 51–52.
[25] Timmons 51–52.
[26] *See* Macklin.

References

Beauchamp, T.L., Standing on Principles : Collected Essays, Oxford University Press, Incorporated, 2010.

Beauchamp, T.L. & Childress, J.F. (2013). Principles of biomedical ethics (7th ed.). New York: Oxford University Press.

Belmont Report: Ethical principles and guidelines for the protection of human subjects of research. National Commission for the Protection of Human Subjects of Biomedical and Behavioral Research. (1979). U.S. Department of Health and Human Services, available at https://www.hhs.gov/ohrp/regulations-and-policy/belmont-report/read-the-belmont-report/index.html

Chambers, T. (2001). The fiction of bioethics: A précis. *American Journal of Bioethics, 1*(1), 40–43.

Emanuel E.J. & Thompson D. (2008), Concept of Conflicts of interest in Medical Research: Historical Developments in The Oxford Textbook of Clinical Research Ethics, 760 (Emanuel E. at el. ed. Oxford).

Gilligan, C. (1982), *In a Different Voice: Psychological Theory and Women's Development*, Cambridge, MA: Harvard University Press.

Goodwin, M. (2020). Policing the Womb. In Policing the Womb: Invisible Women and the Criminalization of Motherhood. Cambridge: Cambridge University Press.

Jasanoff, S. (2016). *The Ethics of Invention: Technology and the Human Future* (1st Ed.) W.W. Norton & Company.

Jonsen AR. Casuistry as methodology in clinical ethics. Theor Med. 1991 Dec ;12(4):295–307.

Kant, I. (2015). The Good Will and the Categorical Imperative, in Shaffer-Landau, R. *The Ethical Life: Fundamental readings in ethics and moral problems* (3rd ed.) (87–99). New York: Oxford University Press.

King, L. Autonomy, Regulation, and Clinical Duties: Balancing Values, Hastings Center Report (November 24, 2017)

Luna Z. and Luker K. Reproductive Justice. Annual Review of Law and Social Science. 2013;9(1):327–52.

Macklin, R. (1999). Against Relativism. Cultural Diversity and the Search for Ethical Universals in Medicine. New York: Oxford University Press.

Munson, R. (2008). "Reproductive Control." Intervention and Reflection: Basic Issues in Medical Ethics. 8th ed. Belmont, CA. 364–451

Norlock, Kathryn, *Feminist Ethics*, Stanford Encyclopedia of Philosophy (2019), available at https://plato.stanford.edu/entries/feminism-ethics/

O'Neill O (2002). *Autonomy and trust in bioethics*. Cambridge: Cambridge University Press.

O'Neill O. *Some limits of informed consent. J Med Ethics* 2003 291, available at https://www.ncbi.nlm.nih.gov/pmc/articles/PMC1733683/pdf/v029p00004.pdf.

Percival, T. (1803), Medical Ethics; or a Code of Institutes and Precepts, Adapted to the Professional Interests of Physicians and Surgeons (Manchester: S. Russell).

Ross, W.D. (1930, Reprinted 2007), The Right and The Good. New York: Oxford University Press

Sandel, Michael (2010). Justice: What's the Right Thing to Do? Farrar, Straus and Giroux; Reprint edition.

Scully, J., *Feminist Bioethics*, Stanford Encyclopedia of Philosophy (Rev 2015), available at https://plato.stanford.edu/entries/feminist-bioethics/.

Sister Song – Reproductive Justice, https://www.sistersong.net/reproductive-justice.

The Oxford Handbook of Reproductive Ethics. Oxford University Press. January 2016.

Timmons, M. (2013). Moral Theory: An introduction (2nd ed.). Lanham, MD: Rowman & Littlefield.

Emerging Reproductive Technologies: Regulating Into the Void

Judith Daar

Abstract This chapter offers an overview of the American legal landscape surrounding assisted reproductive technologies (ART). The three basic sources of law are set out, explaining how constitutional law, statutory law and case law regulate the use of assisted conception. Historically, protection of ART as a constitutional right has been questionable, but grows more uncertain in the wake of the U.S. Supreme Court's decision ending constitutional protection for abortion rights. Congress has paid scant attention to assisted conception as a method of family formation, weighing in only to enact a reporting scheme that collects annual data. Federal legislative efforts have instead been directed at prohibiting the U.S. government from funding any research in which human embryos are created or destroyed, quelling research progress in areas such as germline genome editing and mitochondrial replacement therapy. The bulk of ART regulation is contained in state law that addresses a host of issues, including the parental status of ART offspring, the legality of surrogate parenting arrangements, the division of embryos upon divorce, and the penalties for gametes misdirection and misappropriation. Looking ahead, emerging reproductive technologies may struggle to find solid support in a comprehensive legal regime given the prevailing scattershot approach favored by American lawmakers.

Reproductive medicine is no stranger to controversy and upheaval but appeared wholly unprepared for the shockwave that descended in November 2018 when a Chinese scientist announced to an international audience in Hong Kong that he had edited the germline genome of twin girls born earlier that year. Dr. He Jiankui's revelation that he employed CRISPR-Cas9 technology to alter the DNA in embryos in order to provide HIV-resistance to the resulting offspring unleashed a worldwide

J. Daar (✉)
Northern Kentucky University, Chase College of Law, Highland Heights, KY, USA

© The Author(s), under exclusive license to Springer Nature Switzerland AG 2023
L. P. King, I. C. Band (eds.), *Case Studies in the Ethics of Assisted Reproduction*, https://doi.org/10.1007/978-3-031-41215-8_2

firestorm over the lack of regulation on these medico-techno frontiers.[1] While some of the debate questioned the practical functionality of any prescriptive regulatory schema in the face of vainglorious mad scientists, a healthy discussion roiled over the extent and need for regulation of current and emerging reproductive technologies.[2] While hardly a novel debate, the question of law's role in medically-assisted conception is worthy of description and review so that stakeholders can navigate the inevitable next advance armed with some familiarity with the surrounding landscape.[3] This chapter offers a brief overview of the U.S. approach to regulating reproductive technologies, fully recognizing the limited impact a single nation's law can have on scientific processes untethered by geographic boundaries.

In broad strokes, American law governing reproductive medicine splays into three broad categories – constitutional law (broad principles set out in the federal and state constitutions), enacted law (legislation passed by Congress and state elected bodies) and case law (judicial decisions by federal and state judges).[4] Each source of law plays a role in the regulation of assisted reproductive technologies (ART). In some instances, the law is direct and intentionally aimed at permitting, controlling or proscribing conduct within the ambit of reproductive medicine. In other instances, law is applied by analogy because of its perceived compatibility with the conduct or policy at issue. Increasingly, ART is the subject of specific law as it gains a foothold in family formation. Today, 3 of every 100 births in the United States are attributable to assisted conception, making ART a far more common

---

[1] Henry T. Greely, *CRISPR'd Babies: Human Germline Genome Editing in the 'He Jiankui Affair'*, 6 J. LAW AND THE BIOSCIENCES 111 (2019). CRISPR stands for clustered regularly interspaced short palindromic repeats. Simply put, CRISPR is a genome editing (also called gene editing) technology that give scientists the ability to change an organism's DNA by allowing genetic material to be added, removed, or altered at particular locations in the genome. Potentially, this gene editing technology could be used to knock out or replace segments of DNA that are associated with disease, thus promoting the health of the organism. When used in gametes or embryos, CRISPR would make alterations in the resulting offspring and thus potentially pass from one generation to the next. *See* National Institutes of Health, U.S. National Library of Medicine, Genetics Home Reference, *What are Genome Editing and CRISPR-Cas9?*, https://ghr.nlm.nih.gov/primer/genomicresearch/genomeediting. Professor Greely observes, "This possibility (though not certainty) of intentionally altering descendants' genes is what most upsets many people when it comes to editing the genes of early-stage embryos. By changing an early embryo, the method seeks to change *every* cell in any resulting child." Greely at 114.

[2] *See, e.g.,* Jon Cohen, *New Call to Ban Gene-Edited Babies Divides Biologists*, SCIENCE (Mar. 13, 2019), https://www.sciencemag.org/news/2019/03/new-call-ban-gene-edited-babies-divides-biologists

[3] For example, in an early case challenging the legality of a surrogate parenting contract, the New Jersey Supreme Court relied on adoption law to invalidate the agreement as violative of the birth mother's right to change her mind after birth of the child. In the Matter of Baby M, 109 N.J. 396, 537 A.2d 1227 (1988).

[4] An important omitted category is regulation set out by administrative agencies, most notably in the case of reproductive medicine by the Food & Drug Administration and the National Institutes of Health. These governing regulations are discussed under the category of federal legislation.

practice than neonatal adoption.[5] The assortment of rights and liabilities attendant to the players and practices is vast, ranging from gestational carriers, egg donors, pre-conception sex selection, frozen embryo disputes and sperm-swapping physicians to name a few.

What follows is a foray into the legal landscape governing reproductive medicine organized along the three broad categories that shape the field – constitutional law, federal law and state law. Once the basic framework is set out, each section will briefly consider the suitability of existing legal regimes to address emerging repro-ductive technologies, such as germline genome editing now at the forefront of global debate. With the obvious caveat that U.S. law does not and cannot regulate medical and scientific practices worldwide, the question plumbed is whether current American law is suited to address the development and usage of nascent and future technologies that alter the manner in which human life is formed. The answer is twofold. In the realm of the legal status of ART children, parents and collaborators, the law is its most robust and suitably prepared to incorporate the next generation of medically-assisted offspring. But in the area of supporting and advancing new reproductive technologies and research, U.S. law lags, creating a void into which American scientists increasingly and regrettably are prevented from venturing.

Constitutional Law: Silent But Looming

Put succinctly, the U.S. constitution is old, short and hard to change. Originally framed in the summer of 1787 by delegates to the Constitutional Convention, this foundational document is more a blueprint for the allocation of governmental pow-ers and the protection of individual rights than it a detailed manual clarifying the

---

[5] According to the National Council for Adoption, there were 18,395 domestic infant adoptions in the U.S. in 2014, representing 0.5% of all live births for that year. *See* National Council for Adoption, *Adoption: By the Numbers* (Feb. 15, 2017), https://www.adoptioncouncil.org/publica-tions/2017/02/adoption-by-the-numbers. According to an annual report published by the Centers for Disease Control and Prevention (CDC), in 2019 there were 83,946 children born in the U.S. who were conceived using some form of assisted reproductive technology (ART), defined essentially by the CDC as IVF. *See* Ctrs. for Disease Control & Prevention, U.S. Dep't. of Health and Hum. Servs., 2019 Assisted Reproductive Technology: National Summary Report 25 (2021) (hereafter 2019 ART Report), https://www.cdc.gov/art/reports/2019/pdf/2019-Report-ART-Fertil-ity-Clinic-National-Summary-h.pdf. In addition to IVF births, it is estimated that 60,000 children are born annually via artificial insemination by donor (AID). *See*. Inst. for Sci., Law & Tech. Working Group, *ART Into Science: Regulation of Fertility Techniques*, 281 SCIENCE 651 (1998) (reporting 60,000 AID births annually). Births via IVF and AID bring the total number of children born through assisted conception to roughly 144,000; the total birth rate for 2019 was nearly four million. *See* Ctrs. for Disease Control & Prevention, U.S. Dep't. of Health & Hum. Servs. *Births: Provisional Data for 2019*, Vital Statistics Rapid Release, May 2020, https://www.cdc.gov/nchs/data/vsrr/vsrr-8-508.pdf (reporting 3,745,540 live births in the U.S. in 2019, down by approxi-mately 1% from 2018). Thus, total ART births in the U.S. in 2019 comprised nearly 4% of all live births.

limits and parameters of state action.[6] Unsurprisingly, none of the constitution's 7591 words (the main document plus 27 amendments) reference reproduction or medicine, and certainly do not touch on these concepts combined. Yet the vagaries of this sacrosanct and enduring text arguably give advantage to contemporary application of the constitution's scarce word count as the role of government grows increasingly complex in modern society. In the context of reproductive technologies, interactions between ART and the constitution have been more anticipated than actual. While scholars have opined for decades how the U.S. Supreme Court might address constitutional challenges to laws regulating assisted conception, to date the high court's record on this subject traces to a single World War II-era case.

In 1942, the Court handed down its decision in *Skinner v. Oklahoma*,[7] a case in which thrice-convicted armed robber Jack Skinner challenged the constitutionality of the Oklahoma Habitual Criminal Sterilization Act of 1935, a law passed during the early twentieth-century American eugenics movement.[8] The law authorized state officials to sexually sterilize those convicted two or more times for felony offenses involving "moral turpitude." The statute's impetus was the then *de rigueuer* thinking that virtually all human behavior was heritable and thus removing some "ne'er-do-wells" from the gene pool would improve the human race moving forward. Justice William O. Douglas wrote the unanimous opinion for the Court, overturning the law and describing the case as "touch[ing] a sensitive and important area of human rights...the right to have offspring."[9] Justice Douglas further advanced that "[p]rocreation involves one of the basic civil rights of man...fundamental to the very existence and survival of the race."[10]

The fascination with *Skinner* today by reproductive medicine practitioners and scholars is that it remains the only time the Supreme Court has weighed into the quagmire of constitutional rights surrounding procreation as an affirmative, intentional act. While ample high court and high profile activity attends the negative rights surrounding reproduction – through the use of contraception and abortion – questions about the state's role in limiting or facilitating a person's right to form a family through natural or assisted conception are relegated to a broad midcentury proclamation of reproduction as a fundamental right. At that time, the Court's worldview about where babies come from could not venture beyond the closed two-party union of a biological mother and father, leaving us to wonder how today's

---

[6] *See generally,* Erwin Chemerinsky, CONSTITUTIONAL LAW: PRINCIPLES AND POLICIES (6th ed. 2019).

[7] Skinner v. Oklahoma, 316 U.S. 535 (1942). For a thorough description and analysis of the events and implications surrounding the *Skinner* case, *see* Victoria F. Norse, IN RECKLESS HANDS: SKINNER V. OKLAHOMA AND THE NEAR-TRIUMPH OF AMERICAN EUGENICS (2008).

[8] For a fuller discussion of the American eugenics movement and its implications for reproductive freedom, *see* Judith Daar, THE NEW EUGENICS: SELECTIVE BREEDING IN AN ERA OF REPRODUCTIVE TECHNOLOGIES (2017); Paul A. Lombardo, THREE GENERATIONS, NO IMBECILES: EUGENICS, THE SUPREME COURT AND BUCK V. BELL (2008).

[9] 316 U.S. at 536.

[10] *Id.* at 541.

multi-party, medically-aided configurations would fare as a constitutional matter. Arguments flare on many sides, with some making the case that the *Skinner*-protected right to reproduce includes the myriad choices about when, whether and how to become a parent in the modern era.[11] Others highlight the thin reed that *Skinner* offers, dismiss its applicability to modern forms of assisted conception and urge a more comprehensive accounting for all the stakeholders in the ART equation.[12]

The Court's silence on constitutional protections surrounding family formation via assisted conception is fairly pervasive throughout the judiciary. Since the introduction of IVF in the late 1970s, only a handful of courts have weighed in on whether laws that touch on assisted conception violate constitutional protections traditionally reserved for coital reproduction. For example, in *Lifchez v. Hartigan*, reproductive medicine physicians challenged a provision in an Illinois abortion law, arguing it potentially subjected them to criminal liability for offering IVF to their patients. The court agreed, holding that IVF falls "within a woman's zone of privacy as recognized in *Roe v. Wade*."[13] Discounting any distinction between negative and positive rights surrounding reproduction, the court observed "[i]t takes no leap of logic to see that within the cluster of constitutionally protected choices that includes the right to have access to contraception, there must be included within that cluster the right to submit to a medical procedure that may bring about, rather than prevent, pregnancy."[14] Other courts have expressly dispensed with legal status distinctions between natural and assisted conception, in one case finding no "legal, ethical or logical reason" to treat *in vivo* and *in intro* fertilization differently, adding "[f]rom a propositional standpoint it matters little whether the ovum/sperm union takes place in the private darkness of a fallopian tube or the public glare of a petri dish."[15]

Determining the protection or lack thereof that prospective parents enjoy from government interference with their right to reproduce via ART occurs largely in a legal vacuum. Laws that do arguably impact access or use of reproductive technologies have generally not drawn constitutional challenge in the realm of interference

---

[11] *See, e.g.*, John A. Robertson, CHILDREN OF CHOICE: FREEDOM AND THE NEW REPRODUCTIVE TECHNOLOGIES (1994) (arguing the right to procreate via ART is constitutionally equal to right attached to natural conception and childbirth); Sonia M. Suter, *The "Repugnance" Lens of Gonzales v. Carhart and Other Theories of Reproductive Rights: Evaluating Advanced Reproductive Technologies*, 76 GEO. WASH. L. REV. 1514 (2008) (finding a right to ART potentially supported by theories based on procreative liberty and autonomy, equality and family privacy).

[12] *See, e.g.*, Radhika Rao, *Constitutional Misconceptions*, 93 MICH. L. REV. 1473 (1995) (rejecting the presumptive primacy of procreative liberty as applied to ART, noting that other constitutional rights may be at issue when donors or surrogates are used and their rights need to be taken into relative account); Ann MacLean Massie, *Regulating Choice: A Constitutional Law Response to Professor John A. Robertson's Children of Choice*, 52 WASH. & LEE L. REV. 135 (1995) (expressing concern that constitutionally equalizing coital and noncoital means of reproduction might suppress the interests of resulting offspring).

[13] Lifchez v. Hartigan, 735 F. Supp. 1361 (N.D. Ill. 1990).
[14] *Id.*
[15] Kass v. Kass, 1995 WL 110368 (Sup. Ct. of Nassau Co., NY 1995).

with reproductive freedom. A few exceptions do pepper the landscape, mostly centering on state laws that limit the rights of intended parents in surrogate parenting arrangements. For example, a federal court in Utah struck down a state law voiding surrogate parenting arrangements and declaring "the surrogate mother is the mother of the child for all legal purposes, and her husband, if she is married, is the father of the child for all legal purposes."[16] In *J.R. v. Utah*, the court held that the prohibitory surrogacy law violated the intended parents' "fundamental constitutionally protected liberty interest" to raise the children they have conceived (via IVF).[17] Additionally, the court found that the Utah law violated equal protection of the law by permitting the intended father to be listed on a surrogate-born child's birth certificate in certain cases but prohibiting the intended mother to be listed in all cases.[18] While constitutional challenges to the validity of surrogate parenting arrangements are sparse, virtually all have resolved in favor of the intended parents' rights to enjoy a parent-child relationship with the offspring born of those agreements.[19]

Challenges to ART regulation based on constitutional violation could also cluster around the authority of Congress or a state legislature to enact such a law in the first place. This powers question, like that of infringement with individual rights, has essentially never been effectively advanced. As discussed in Section "Federal law: Regulating reporting, restricting research", the federal government's legislative activity on ART regulation is extant but sparse. In the instances in which Congress has enacted a reproductive medicine-related law, its authority to do so seemed settled (or at least unchallenged). For example, in 2005 the Food & Drug Administration promulgated regulations governing the use of donated reproductive tissue, i.e., sperm, eggs and embryos. The regulations set up good tissue practice protocols for screening and testing of donors who supplied gametes for reproductive use to avoid disease transmission.[20] In commenting on the federal government's authority to act in this area, one scholar asserts that the Commerce Clause of the Constitution provides this power by virtue of ART's reach across state borders and via the internet.[21] In his advocacy for greater federal regulation of donor reproductive tissue, Professor Yaniv Heled argues that the authority to establish national standards in the practice of medicine – an area that has traditionally been regulated by the states – is grounded

---

[16] J.R. v. Utah, 261 F. Supp. 2d 1268 (D. Utah 2002). *See also* Soos v. Superior Court in and for County of Maricopa, 182 Ariz. 470 (1994) (declaring provision of state law that named surrogate and her husband as legal parents unconstitutional).

[17] 261 F. Supp. at 1296.

[18] Id. at 1294.

[19] *See, e.g.,* Johnson v. Calvert, 5 Cal. 4th 87, 98–99 (1993) (finding no constitutional rights of a gestational carrier are implicated by upholding the intended parents' legal rights because she is not considered a legal mother of any child born).

[20] Food & Drug Administration, Guidance for Industry, Eligibility Determination for Donors of Human Cells, Tissues, and Cellular and Tissue-Based Products, 69 F.R. 29,786–01 (May 25, 2004).

[21] Yaniv Heled, *The Regulation of Genetic Aspects of Donated Reproductive Tissue – The Need for Federal Regulation*, 11 COL. SCIENCE & TECH. L. REV. 243, 297 (2010). The Commerce Clause of the U.S. Constitution gives Congress the authority "To regulate Commerce… among the several States." U.S. Const., Art. I, Sec. 8.

in the recognized ability of the federal government to set uniform national standards for health and safety.[22] The viability of this argument is now more questionable, given it was advanced before the Supreme Court weighed in disapprovingly on the Commerce Clause as a basis for Congress' authority to regulate in the health insurance arena.[23]

Looking ahead, the constitutionality of any enacted law that touches on ART may depend upon the status of the negative right surrounding reproduction – the right to abortion. For nearly 50 years, the right to obtain an abortion prior to fetal viability was considered constitutionally protected under two prevailing U.S. Supreme Court decisions. In 1973, the U.S. Supreme Court held in *Roe v. Wade* that the Fourteenth Amendment's concept of personal liberty protected individual decision-making related to pregnancy termination.[24] In 1992, the U.S. Supreme Court reaffirmed the core holding in *Roe*, setting out the prevailing standard for evaluating state action on abortion, balancing a woman's interest in procreative liberty against the state's interest in the life of the unborn. In *Planned Parenthood of Southeastern Pennsylvania v. Casey,* the Court held that regulation will be invalid if it poses an "undue burden" on the right of a woman to decide whether to terminate a pregnancy. An undue burden exists, "if its purpose or effect is to place a substantial obstacle in the path of a woman seeking an abortion before the fetus attains viability."[25]

In June 2022, *Roe* and *Casey* were overturned in *Dobbs v. Jackson Women's Health Organization*, a 6–3 Supreme Court decision holding the Constitution does not confer a right to obtain an abortion, leaving regulation of pregnancy termination up to individual states.[26] The majority opinion in *Dobbs* addresses concerns that the decision leaves other types of personal decision-making vulnerable to restrictive regulation, including access to contraception and same-sex marriage. Writing for the Court, Justice Alito says that other rights are not impacted because they do not involve "potential life."[27] This reassurance is of little solace to those concerned about access to IVF, a technique in which early embryos are often discarded at patient direction. Routine aspect of IVF, including preimplantation genetic testing and embryo cryopreservation may be subject to restriction in a post-*Roe* world as the balance of state interests shifts from protecting patient choice and autonomy to

---

[22] *Id.* at 297, citing Gonzales v. Oregon, 546 U.S. 243 (2006), in which the Supreme Court acknowledged the federal government's authority to set uniform standards in the regulation of health and safety.

[23] *See* National Federation of Independent Business v. Sebelius, 567 U.S. 519 (2012) (a majority of the Court finding that the Affordable Care Act's individual mandate to purchase health insurance was not a valid exercise of Congress' power to regulate commerce; the Commerce Clause allows Congress to regulate existing commercial activity, but not to compel individuals to participate in commerce).

[24] 410 U.S. 113 (1973).

[25] 505 U.S. 833, 878 (1992).

[26] 597 U.S. __ (2022).

[27] Id. at __.

favoring unborn human life over any other interests.[28] As of this writing, the *Dobbs* impact on abortion access in the U.S., let alone its derivative impact on assisted conception, is unknown but the Court has given more freedom to lawmakers to place restrictions on activity that touches on early human life. How might this new freedom impact emerging technologies that are still in the development stage?

For example, if Congress were to enact a law that prohibited researchers from pursing and patients from access germline genome editing technologies, would this pass constitutional muster? Setting aside the scientist's claim of interference with protected First Amendment rights of free expression, the patient argument – still relying on a *Casey* framework – would assert that such a prohibition imposes an undue burden on the protected liberty interest to access the means necessary to conceive a healthy child. In whatever manner a person chooses to procreate (i.e., with whom, by whatever means), the argument might go, that choice should be free from state interference. Any prohibition on access to germline gene editing would amount to an undue burden in the path of a prospective parent seeking to navigate their reproductive journey, a core and constitutionally protected human experience. This barebones assertion plucks selectively from broad language in *Skinner* and *Casey*, combining tenets of constitutional law that are tenuous in isolation and thus highly fallible in combination. Application of the current *Dobbs* rubric further weakens such an assertion, as the new standard shifts the focus solidly toward the state's interest in protecting potential life from harmful experimentation. Courts will be much freer to uphold laws restricting reproductive choice as long as lawmakers can surmount a minimal threshold of concern for health and safety impacts.

Assuming arguendo that use of advanced germline technologies is included in some surviving basket of protected reproductive rights, the assertion of unfettered access is far too simplistic and would give way to standardized balancing of individual and governmental interests. As a general matter, individual constitutional rights are not absolute and must be balanced against compelling state interests that motivated the enacted restrictions. The nascency and uncertainty surrounding emerging reproductive technologies, including technologies that fundamentally alter natural genetic inheritance patterns, weigh heavily in favor of the government's authority to act. Until safety and efficacy levels achieve some modicum of reliability – possibly involving at least two generations of subjects because of the heritable nature of the genetic alterations – the government's interest in protecting human health would likely outweigh a parent's interest in birthing a child in this manner. Virtually every organization involved in the field has either called for a permanent moratorium on continued research or counseled against proceeding until safety and efficacy are more firmly established.[29] Query whether U.S.-based data on safety and efficacy surrounding emerging reproductive technologies will ever materialize to tip

---

[28] I. Glenn Cohen, Judith Daar, Eli Adashi, *What Overturning Roe v. Wade May Mean for Assisted Reproductive Technologies in the U.S.*, 328(1) JAMA 15–16 (June 6, 2022).

[29] *See* Ethics in Embryo Research Task Force and Ethics Committee of the American Society for Reproductive Medicine, *Ethics in Embryo Research*, 113 Fertil. Steril 270 (2020).

the balance in favor of patients' rights, given the restrictive regulatory environment enveloping such activity, as explored below.

Federal Law: Regulating Reporting, Restricting Research

The system of federalism in the U.S. means that elected representatives at both the federal and state levels have authority to enact law – with an intricate constitutional overlay governing exclusivity of subject matter and questions of preemption. Congress, at the federal level, has taken up this legislative authority rather sparingly in the field of reproductive medicine. Lawmakers in state capitols have displayed more interest in regulating conduct surrounding assisted reproduction, in part because the areas ripe for legal input are traditional areas of state law such as family law, tort law and schemes governing inheritance. Public policy and localized preferences play a major role in state lawmaking, yielding a proverbial checkerboard of jurisprudence governing ART when viewed from a nationwide perspective. Not infrequently, regional and state-by-state differences give rise to reproductive tourism, where intended parents and their collaborators travel across state lines to access a more permissive legal regime than exists in their state of domicile. With this rough sketch of federal and state spheres of authority, one can build a clearer picture of ART laws across the country. Looking first at federal law, the picture is one of two distinct buckets – one establishing a comprehensive national reporting scheme for patient IVF usage, the other a restrictive framework impeding scientific advancement in the research realm.

Federal Law Governing Clinical Fertility Practice

Congress has concerned itself with reproductive technologies in two broad categories – (1) laws regulating the delivery and reporting of medical services aimed at family formation, and (2) laws governing federal funding for research in reproductive medicine. In the former category, two main federally-based regulatory schemes impact the clinical practice of ART in the U.S. The first federal law governing the practice of infertility medicine was enacted in 1992 in response to reports that IVF clinics were inflating their pregnancy rates in order to attract patients.[30] The Fertility Clinic Success Rate and Certification Act (FCSRCA) requires infertility medicine service providers to report success rates and related data in an effort to improve transparency and enhance consumer/patient protection.[31] As a result of this

---

[30] *See Fertility Clinic Services: Hearings Before the Subcomm. On Health and the Env't of the H. Comm. On Energy & Com.,* 102d Cong. 1–2 (1992) (testimony revealing deception by some fertility clinics to inflate treatment success rates).

[31] 42 U.S.C. 263a-1 (1992).

mandate, in 1997 the Centers for Disease Control began what is now an annual collection and publication of ART data, including clinic specific and national summaries on patient diagnosis, number of embryos transferred, pregnancy and live-birth rates.[32] Despite comprehensive annual reporting, critique of this federal law is ample. Lingering concerns remain over the "cherry picking" of patients in order to manipulate higher pregnancy rates as well as the law's tepid enforcement provision – a mere listing at the end of each report of known clinics that did not report data.[33]

A second federal ART actor is the Food and Drug Administration, charged with protecting the public health by assuring the safety, efficacy, and security of drugs, medical devices and biological products, including human gametes.[34] In 2005, the FDA issued comprehensive regulations requiring tissue banks to test gamete donors and donated tissues for a host of infectious communicable diseases, as well as requiring donors to answer a series of questions to determine their risk factors for particular diseases.[35] The prevalence of egg donation in IVF – hovering at around 12% of all cycles, coupled with the tens of thousands of sperm donor births, combine to magnify the import of proper screening and testing of donor gametes to assure child and maternal health and safety.[36]

The FDA regulatory scheme, like FCSRCA, weathers critique about its effectiveness and usefulness for patients and offspring. The main flaw, many argue, is the omission of genetic screening and testing of gamete donors and tissue.[37] In response, the reproductive medicine community often points to the industry's self-regulation, embodied in large part in guidelines issued by the American Society for Reproductive Medicine – the largest professional organization for reproductive medicine specialists in the world. The ASRM practice guidelines for gamete and embryo donation do recommend genetic evaluation and testing for all egg, sperm and embryos donors.[38] Studies suggest the degree to which donor egg and sperm purveyors (banks and individual practices) adhere to recommended genetic testing is variable,

---

[32] 42 U.S.C. §263a-1 et seq.

[33] See Lucy Frith & Eric Blyth, *Assisted Reproductive Technology in the USA: Is More Regulation Needed?* 29 REPRODUCTIVE BIOMEDICINE ONLINE 516 (2014).

[34] For a history of the FDA's authority over ART, *see* Judith Daar, *Federalizing Embryo Transfer: Taming the Wild West of Reproductive Medicine?*, 23 COL. J. GENDER & LAW 257, 269 (2012).

[35] Human Cells, Tissues, and Cellular and Tissue-Based Products, 21 C.F.R. §1271, https://www.fda.gov/vaccines-blood-biologics/tissue-tissue-products/donor-eligibility-final-rule-and-guidance-questions-and-answers

[36] *See supra* note 5 (2019 ART Report reporting approximately 27,000 of the 200,000 IVF cycles involved donor eggs).

[37] *See* Frith & Blyth, *supra* note 33. *See also* Held, *supra* note 21.

[38] Practice Committee of the American Society for Reproductive Medicine, *Recommendations for Gamete and Embryo Donation: A Committee Opinion*, 99 FERTIL STERIL 47 (2013).

and thus insufficiently robust to protect stakeholders from transmission of genetic anomalies via collaborative reproduction.[39]

The lack of comprehensive, top-down regulation of ART practice in the U.S. is regularly and starkly contrasted with regimes in other countries in which licensing of clinical practice and individual clinics is strictly controlled. Federally deployed schemes in the UK and Canada create national norms and practices, arguably enabling a swifter and unified response to emerging technologies.[40] Putting aside the dim likelihood that Congress could sufficiently align to enact a comprehensive federal regulatory scheme to govern reproductive medicine, earlier indications are that they expressly eschewed this opportunity. A provision in FCSRCA enables the CDC to establish a model program for the certification of embryo labs. However, in so doing, the law admonishes, "In developing the certification program, the Secretary may not establish any regulation, standard, or requirement which has the effect of exercising supervision or control over the practice of medicine in assisted reproductive technology programs."[41] When this language was drafted in 1992, Congress may have been concerned about its authority under the Commerce Clause to regulate in the health law arena, traditionally regarded as within the states' authority a part "of that immense mass of legislation...not surrendered to a general [federal] government."[42] Whatever the legal or policy rationale for Congress stepping away from regulating the practice and delivery of infertility care, a new enthusiasm for tamping down emerging technologies has entered the regulatory landscape. Newly developing reproductive techniques provoke attention in the research arena, to which we now turn.

Federal Law Regulating ART Research

Until somewhat recently, advances in IVF and ancillary techniques to assist conception and pregnancy were developed without much, if any, regulatory oversight. Enhancements to IVF such as intracytoplasmic sperm injection (ICSI) – which aids fertilization by injecting a single sperm into the oocyte, and preimplantation genetic testing (PGT) – which reveals the genetic make-up of early embryos to assess the

---

[39] *See, e.g.,* R.M. Lim, P. Callum, C. Ruberto, R.E. Zinberg,
   Genetic Screening Practices at Ooocyte Donation Programs, 96 FERTIL. STERIL. S218 (2011) (reporting industry guidelines for genetic testing inconsistently implemented at oocyte donation programs).

[40] The Human Fertilisation and Embryology Act (1990, updated 2008) governs ART in the UK, *see* http://www.legislation.gov.uk/ukpga/2008/22/contents; in Canada, the Assisted Human Reproduction Act (2004) governs. *See* https://www.canada.ca/en/health-canada/services/drugs-health-products/biologics-radiopharmaceuticals-genetic-therapies/legislation-guidelines/assisted-human-reproduction.html

[41] 42 U.S.C. §263a-2(i).

[42] U.S. v. Lopez, 514 U.S. 549, 594 (quoting Gibbons v. Ogden, 22 U.S. 1, 203 (1824)).

future child's health, were developed in the 1990s and gradually became fully integrated into clinical care without provoking oversight or objection by federal (or state) regulators.[43] But in 2001, the U.S. regulatory sleeping giant stirred, and became fully awake in 2015 as scientists progressed to develop techniques that – while therapeutic in intent - had the potential to alter the human genome in perpetuity. The notion of germline alteration and its ability to imbue heritable changes in the genome struck some as a step too far, thus unleashing opposition to further research at the highest levels.[44]

First on the modern germline-editing scene, mitochondrial replacement therapy (MRT) is aimed at preventing the transmission of mitochondrial disease from mother to child by replacing the cytoplasm of an affected woman's egg cell with that from a healthy donor egg. The result is an egg with the nucleus from the intended mother (which contains the vast majority of DNA) and the cytoplasm – including mitochondria or organelles that power the cell – of a healthy donor. Mitochondria contains a small amount of DNA (less than 0.1% of the entire amount found in the egg cell), thus any resulting child will have DNA from three individuals (the intended mother, the egg donor and the biological father).[45] The seeming unnaturalness of this parental triad spurred the FDA to take action, essentially prohibiting any research or clinical activity surrounding MRT.

The FDA pathway was to assert jurisdiction over the use of cytoplasmic transfer and prohibit clinical trials until investigators filed an investigational new drug application (IND).[46] According to federal regulations, biological products (including

---

[43] See generally Michelle Bayefsy, Who Should Regulate Preimplantation Genetic Diagnosis in the United States? AMA JOURNAL OF ETHICS (Dec. 2018), https://journalofethics.ama-assn.org/article/who-should-regulate-preimplantation-genetic-diagnosis-united-states/2018-12;

[44] In 2015, Francis Collins, the Director of the National Institutes of Health issued a statement announcing that NIH would not fund any use of gene-editing technologies in human embryos, adding, "The concept of altering the human germline in embryos for clinical purposes has been debated over many years from many different perspectives, and has been viewed almost universally as a line that should not be crossed." Francis Collins, Statement on NIH Funding of Research Using Gene-Editing Technologies in Human Embryos (Apr. 28, 2015), https://www.nih.gov/about-nih/who-we-are/nih-director/statements/statement-nih-funding-research-using-gene-editing-technologies-human-embryos

[45] See Rosa J. Castro, Mitochondrial Replacement Therapy: The UK and US Regulatory Landscapes, 3 J. LAW & BIOSCIENCES 726 (2016).

[46] Normally, all new drugs and biological products are required to be reviewed by the FDA before they are eligible for clinical use. Occasionally, the FDA will receive requests to allow researchers to administer investigational new drugs (those which have yet been approved) to humans for the purposes of testing the drugs' safety and effectiveness, Federal law (21 U.S.C. 355(i) and 42 U.S.C. 262(a)(3)) provides the FDA with authority to grant exemptions from review in these situations. See https://scipol.duke.edu/track/consolidated-appropriations-act-2016-public-law-114-113. The IND link to MRT is explained by the National Academies of Science, Engineering and Medicine as follows: "Human genome-editing technologies are considered to be gene therapies with regard to FDA oversight, and the agency regulates human genome editing under the existing framework for biological products, which includes gene therapy products." National Academies of Sciences, Engineering, and Medicine; National Academy of Medicine; National Academy of Sciences; Committee on Human Gene Editing: Scientific, Medical, and Ethical

gene therapy products) may be used in humans during their development only if an IND application is in effect.[47] This massive hoop put an end to early uses of MRT in the 1990s and early 2000s, but improvements in the technique (reported mostly by researchers outside the US) saw the federal government take an even more aggressive stance against germline manipulation. In December 2015, Congress enacted a renewable provision of the Consolidated Appropriation Act of 2016 forestalling the prospect of human germline modification which includes both MRT and emerging techniques used to edit embryos.[48] The provision stipulates that "none of the funds made available by this Act [to the FDA] may be used to review or approve an application for an exemption for investigational use of a drug or biological product… in which a human embryo is intentionally created or modified to include a heritable genetic modification"[49] Since 2015, the FDA has been precluded from even acknowledging – let alone acting on – any research proposals to study MRT or germline editing, as the law also provides that any IND in the area "shall be deemed to have not been received by the Secretary [of Health and Human Services]".[50]

To be clear, a federal law that prohibits a federal agency from even reviewing a research protocol is distinct from a void in the regulation of the activity. This void, in which research on human germline genome editing is not expressly illegal but cannot proceed because of the unavailability of administrative review, is quirky but not surprising. Despite considerable concern over the safety, efficacy and ethical challenges posed by the prospect of germline genome editing, Congress has not acted to ban it outright.[51] A similar history of congressional hand-wringing followed by inaction surrounded the introduction of another highly freighted reproductive technology – human cloning. In 1997, after researchers announced the birth of Dolly the Sheep - the world's first cloned mammal, states lined up to ban human cloning. Congress, despite wide rebuke for the possibility of replicating a person's genome in their offspring, never voted to ban the technique (if it were ever to become clinically possible) in the U.S.[52] Instead of banning – or even regulating – conduct in the reproductive technology realm, Congress has taken a more indirect route, but one that has effectively suppressed scientific activity in the field. Congress

---

Considerations, *Human Genome Editing: Science, Ethics, and Governance* (Feb. 2017), https://www.ncbi.nlm.nih.gov/books/NBK447266/

[47] 21 CFR Part 312.

[48] *See* I. Glenn Cohen & Eli Adashi, *The FDA is Prohibited From Going Germline*, 353 SCIENCE 545 (2016).

[49] Pub. Law 113–114, Sec. 749 (2015).

[50] *Id.*

[51] *See* Cohen & Adashi, *supra* note 48 reviewing congressional hearings on the issue of germline editing. Thus, while germline genome research is not illegal per se, it can only be done using private funding and only at the pre-clinical level. Any attempt to transfer an edited egg, sperm or embryo into a human being would require an IND – unattainable under current law.

[52] *See* Judith Daar, *The Prospect of Human Cloning: Improving Nature of Dooming the Species?*, 33 SETON HALL L. REV. 511 (2003) (detailing legislative reactions to cloning, including state bans and the many bills introduced but not passed in Congress).

has exercised its power of the purse to withhold federal funding from nearly all ART research.

Since 1996, federal law has prohibited the U.S. government from funding any research in which a human embryo is created or destroyed. In 1995, Congress passed the Dickey-Wicker Amendment which prohibits the use of U.S. Department of Health and Human Services funds for "creation of a human embryo(s) for research purposes or research in which a human embryo(s) are destroyed, discarded, or knowingly subjected to risk of injury or death for research purposes."[53] Dickey-Wicker was signed into law in 1996 and has been reapproved as part of the federal budget each year thereafter. While not restricting embryo research per se or the use of private funds for embryo research, this amendment significantly curtails embryo research in the U.S. with the absence of the nation's largest source of scientific research funding. Moreover, the FDA's inability to even open a proposal in the mail that proposes certain types of embryo research further delimits progress in understanding, exploring and refining advances in reproductive medicine.

The threads of federal law surrounding ART can appear truly at odds with each other when viewed from a patient health and safety perspective. While the government is heavily invested in the epidemiology of fertility care – measuring each patient visit, procedure and outcome – it is mostly hands off in interacting with the safety and effectiveness of the techniques employed. No federal standards or suggested best practices exist to guide practitioners – even to establish a minimum standard of practice. While patient and child well-being are addressed via the FDA regulations surrounding infectious disease transmission through gamete donation, the greater threat to ART offspring health rests in heritable genetic anomalies passed by egg, sperm and embryo donors. As noted, the FDA has yet to add this category to its testing profile, allowing clinics to fill this lacuna. With respect to emerging technologies, the federal government's aim is clear – any attempt to advance human health by exploring new frontiers in reproductive medicine will be shut down, either by financial strangling or suppressive administrative regimes. While an overarching federal regulatory scheme could be impactful, the bulk of clinical practice dwells under the auspices of state law. This complicated morass reaches many aspects of assisted conception, some of which is described below.

State Law: An Evolving and Growing Landscape

Since the birth of the world's first IVF baby in 1978, the planet has welcomed more than 8 million babies born through the technology.[54] While each birth hopefully sparked joy for the welcoming parents, many brought legal questions that simply

---

[53] The Balanced Budget Downpayment Act, I, Pub L No 103–99; 128, 110 Stat.34 (1996).

[54] *See More than 8 Million Babies Born from IVF Since the World's First in 1978*, SCIENCE DAILY (July 3, 2018), https://www.sciencedaily.com/releases/2018/07/180703084127.htm

did not arise when a child was conceived the old-fashioned way. These questions sort into broad categories of state law, accustomed to resolving family-related dilemmas. IVF-inspired legal matters are diverse, but a few clusters of frequently asked questions include the determination of legal parentage when a gamete or embryo donor is involved, the legality of surrogate parenting arrangements, the disposition of frozen embryos upon divorce, the inheritance rights of children conceived after the death of a genetic parent and the liability of ART practitioners for mishaps (or worse) in the provision of fertility services.[55] While the nature of state law is that each jurisdiction can create its own legal framework for each of these scenarios, often trends and majority positions do emerge. In many instances, we see a slight movement toward national harmonization as family formation via ART becomes increasingly normalized.

Determining the Legal Parentage of Donor-Conceived Children

Early cases adjudicating the legal parentage of donor-conceived children were harsh and inconsistent, prompting the National Conference of Commissioners of Uniform State Laws to promulgate the Uniform Parentage Act (UPA) in 1973.[56] Since revised in 2000, 2002 and 2017, the UPA addresses the parentage of donor-conceived children in simple and direct terms. Sections 702 and 703 provides, "A donor is not a parent of a child conceived by assisted reproduction; An individual who consents…to assisted reproduction by a woman with the intent to be a parent of a child conceived by the assisted reproduction is a parent of the child.[57] The UPA provisions on donor parentage have been adopted in 13 states, and a majority of American jurisdictions have enacted similar laws immunizing a gamete donor from a finding of paternity (though many laws only address sperm donation and not the more recently emerged egg donation).[58] Within this somewhat ethereal overlay recognizing donor nonparentage, individual state laws vary across a handful of factors. Distinctions in the legal treatment of gamete donors depends upon one or more of

---

[55] The latter two topics are not covered in this chapter, but ample commentary is illuminating. *See, e.g.*, Kristine S. Knaplund, *Assisted Reproductive Technology: The Legal Issues*, 28 Prob. & Prop. 48 (2014) (discussing parentage and inheritance rights of post-mortem conceived children); Dov Fox, Birth Rights and Wrongs: How Medicine and Technology are Remaking Reproduction and the Law (2019) (advancing a theory of reproductive negligence for errors, mishaps and wrongdoing in reproductive medicine).

[56] *See. e.g.*, Doornbos v. Doornbos, 139 N.E.2d. 844 (Ill. App. Ct.1956) (use of donor insemination constitutes adultery by wife, child is not legitimate child of marriage); Gursky v. Gursky, 39 Misc. 2d 1083, 242 N.Y.S.2d 406 (1963) (declaring child of sperm donation used during marriage "not the legitimate issue of the husband").

[57] Unif. Parentage Act (Unif. Law Comm'n 2017), §§702–703.

[58] *See* Deborah L. Forman, *Exploring the Boundaries of Families Created with Known Sperm Providers: Who's I and Who's Out*, 19 U. Pa. J.L. & Soc. Change 41 (2016) (cataloging state law regarding parentage of donor-conceived children).

the following factors - marital status (typically of the woman giving birth), the use of a licensed physician (for insemination, as egg donation cannot be achieved DIY), the expressed intent of the parties (most protectively in writing) and the parties' conduct (both before and after the child is conceived).[59] A full plate of court cases interprets statutes in many states, with some laws enacted before the emergence of the technology to which they are being applied.[60] In other instances, courts have no enacted law to rely on, issuing judgments based on local public policy.

Venturing into gamete donation today means understanding the legal subtleties in the jurisdiction where a dispute over parental rights might arise. In states with rulings that a donor can be considered a parent (for example, based on post-birth behavior or lack of a written agreement specifying the gamete provider is a donor),[61] parties wising to avert such a designation might consider the onerous option of relocating or enlisting legal assistance to maximize the possibility that the arrangement's intent is professionally memorialized. Yet even the most assiduous allocation of rights as between gamete providers and intended parents bumps up against another limitation of current jurisprudence – a binary structure in which a party is deemed either a donor or a parent under law. This construction may be ill-suited to address parentage in the coming age of emerging technologies – for example, the advent of in vitro gametogenesis (IVG). Now being tested in mouse models, IVG is the derivation of gametes from an individual's somatic cells (typically skin cells) that have been induced to a pluripotent, or stem, phase and then differentiated into either sperm or egg cells. This technology would enable same-sex couples to conceive offspring who are genetically related to both of them; allow single individuals to procreate without contribution from another person; and facilitate "multiplex" parenting where more than two people procreate together.[62] Adding the further prospect of three-parent children born from mitochondrial replacement therapy and the notion of one person-one parent further devolves.[63]

Thus, while state law might be fulsome in its coverage of parentage dilemmas surrounding donor-conceived children, its agility to adapt to new configurations in reproduction should be addressed. As complex as assisted reproductive appears today, the law's main job is to determine which two individuals should be named as

---

[59] *Id.* at 42–45.

[60] For example, in deciding a dispute between two women who used egg donation to birth a child, the California Supreme Court looked to the state's law on sperm donation as no specific statute addressed the more recently emerged technology. K.M. v. E.G., 37 Cal. 4th 130, 33 Cal. Rptr. 3d 61 (2005).

[61] *See, e.g.,* Jason P. v. Danielle S., 171 Cal. Rptr. 3d 789, 796–97 (Cal. Ct. App. 2014) (recharacterization of sperm provider from donor to parent based on post-birth conduct); Ferguson v. McKiernan, 940 A.2d 1236, 1248 (Pa. 2007) (court adopting opt-out system where sperm providers are considered parents, with full parental rights and responsibilities, unless the provider and recipient expressly agree otherwise).

[62] *See* Sonia M. Suter, *In Vitro Gametogenesis: Just Another Way to Have a Baby?,* 3 J. OF LAW AND THE BIOSCIENCES, 87 (2015).

[63] *See generally* Judith Daar, *Multi-Party Parenting in Genetics and Law: A View From Succession,* 49 FAMILY L. QUARTERLY 71 (2015).

legal parents. A good advance away from mother/father as the only options, a finding of parent 1/parent 2 may not suit a situation in which three (or more) individuals contribute equally to a child's genome. Today's laws are somewhat ill-suited to fully embrace multiplex parenting.[64] On the other end of the parental contributory spectrum, it may be that germline gene editing is perfected to the point where a child bears no genetic relation to the individuals who supplied the egg and sperm. If CRISPR-Cas9 is used to delete the genes that formed in an early embryo naturally through fertilization, only to replace them with synthetically-derived genes, who are the resulting child's parents? Thought experiments along these wild lines include the use of IVG by a single person to derive eggs and sperm which combine into an embryo, only to be altered through gene editing to remove and replace all functional genes with laboratory-based substitutes. While hardly an approaching reality, it behooves us to consider how we might approach these parental deconstructions so that future legal regimes reflect our core family values.

Surrogate Parenting Arrangements in Global Context

An arrangement wherein a woman (or trans man) agrees to gestate an embryo for another person or couple, typically in exchange for compensation, and relinquish the child to the intended rearing parent(s) continues to rise in usage in the U.S.[65] At the same time, acceptance of surrogate parenting arrangements as legally enforceable agreements has swelled over the past 10 years. The national picture 10 years ago revealed about 20% of the states banning (or refusing to enforce) agreements and half of all states maintaining no express law on surrogacy, thus making parties vulnerable to rejection of pre-birth agreements and prompting surrogacy tourism within the U.S. Today the landscape is much changed, with nearly all states favorably regulating or tacitly permitting commercial surrogacy.[66] As a result of growing legal acceptance, surrogacy tourism within the U.S. should logically decline, though third party agencies will likely remain dominant in previously friendly surrogacy locales such as California.[67] While the legal barriers surrounding surrogacy are diminishing in the U.S., cost and other features are driving Americans to seek services outside the country – giving rise to a host of new legal concerns.

---

[64] *Id.* at 75–77 (discussing evolving law on multi-party parenthood).

[65] According to the CDC national report on ART, embryo transfers using a gestational carrier almost quadrupled from 2010 to 2019, moving from 2649 to 9195. *See* 2019 ART Report, *supra* note 5, at 34.

[66] *See* Jenna Casolo, et al., *Assisted Reproductive Technologies*, 20 Geo. J. Gender & Law 313, 330–42 (2019) (reviewing permissive, restrictive and prohibitive jurisdictions in the U.S.). *See also* Updated United States Surrogacy Map, https://www.creativefamilyconnections.com/us-surrogacy-law-map/

[67] *See* Cal. Family Code §7962.

The recent COVID-19 pandemic highlighted the plight of intended parents who travel abroad for surrogacy services. As nation after nation shut down movement within and to their borders, stories emerged about hundreds of babies born to gestational carriers awaiting pick-up by their intended parents whose domicile was outside the jurisdiction. One news story reported that 1000 babies would be born to surrogates in Ukraine during the pandemic whose parents would be unable to enter the country. These stranded infants would eventually find their homes in a host of countries, including the U.S., Italy, Spain, China, France the UK and others, highlighting the globalization of this collaborative reproductive practice.[68] Other legal constraints wrought by the internationalization of surrogacy touch on the child's citizenship and immigration status. Another widely read newspaper story detailed the plight of U.S. gay parents whose daughter was denied citizenship after being born to a surrogate abroad.[69] The convoluted and outdated State Department policy at play, the couple sued the federal department for discrimination based on sexual orientation. These tales of child mobility constraints arising from parental outreach to cross-border carriers strains whatever harmony the U.S. has achieved in the surrogacy arena.

In keeping with the chapter's theme of dilemmas posed by new technologies, consider the parentage of a child gestated in something other than a human uterus. Would the child face the possibility of nonparentage because of the law's requirement for some biologic connection to a birth mother? Should ectogenesis – gestation in an artificial environment outside the body – ever be perfected to acceptable levels of safety and efficacy, will the child be regarded as the product of a gestational carrier – thus, invoking the legal regime surrounding surrogacy? Will the generalized acceptance of surrogacy in the U.S. embrace nonhuman gestation as merely the next step along the reproductive technology chain or will those children face legal hurdles beyond our current comprehension? The prospect of eliminating a birth mother from the procreative equation challenges us to consider the inadequacy of current law to address future developments. Reimagining those laws now can help us prepare for the inevitable next development in technology-aided family formation.

Embryo Disposition Upon Divorce and Relationship Dissolution

The true disruption of IVF was its disaggregation of sex and reproduction, a previous coupling that assured gametes would meld together only within the deep recesses of a woman's body. Retrieving and exposing sperm, egg and embryo to human manipulation in a laboratory invited error, mishaps and disagreement over

---

[68] Andrew E. Kramer, *100 Babies Stranded in Ukraine After Surrogate Births*, NY Times (May 16, 2020).

[69] Sarah Mervosh, *Gay U.S. Couple Sues State Dept. for Denying Their Baby Citizenship*, NY Times (July 23, 2019).

an outcome that natural reproduction never afforded – the disposition of gametes and embryos when their progenitors die or disagree over control. Embryo disputes are most suited for resolution under state law because they largely involve areas almost exclusively governed at the state level – contract law and its application under the jurisdiction's public policy. As a result of this jurisprudential reality, the law has grown on a case by case basis, with a smattering of statutes enacted to set standardized practices within state borders.[70] The legal landscape remains, in the main, somewhat bare as less than half of all states have expressly ruled on how embryos should be distributed upon divorce or dissolution of a nonmarital relationship. While the previously discussed dilemmas over parentage of donor-conceived offspring and enforceability of surrogate parenting agreements are seeing a pathway to harmonization, the allocation of rights in embryo disposition remains variable across the country.

To date, about a quarter of all states have weighed in on the question of embryo disposition upon divorce, overwhelmingly by judicial decision at the appellate level.[71] As commentators have explained, the cases generally adopt one of three approaches to resolve the dispute at hand and guide future disputes: (1) the contract approach (enforce the terms of a pre-existing agreement between the parties); (2) the contemporaneous mutual consent approach (permit disposition only upon agreement of the parities); and (3) the balancing approach (look to a host of factors including each party's opportunity to become a parent without the use of the disputed embryos).[72] Initially, each of these approaches overwhelming favored the party wishing to avoid procreation (nearly universally the male partner), and refused to allow release of the embryos to the wannabe parent (mostly the female partner). This trend continues with one notable line of deviation. In some of the cases in which the female partner wishing to use the embryos has undergone chemotherapy and is no longer able to produce eggs, courts have ruled in favor of the recovered woman.[73] Interestingly, a woman's age-induced infertility has not been regarded in the same way by courts even though a woman of advanced maternal age can be functionally in the same position as a cancer survivor with respect to her ability to become a biologic parent.

---

[70] For example, in Arizona a statute was enacted after a court held that disputed embryos should be awarded to the ex-husband – who wanted to donate them to another couple – based on a written agreement of the parties. The elected official favored a different outcome – one in which the wife would prevail. Thus, the legislature enacted a law effectively abrogating prior agreements and directing courts to award embryos "to the spouse who intends to allow the in vitro human embryos to develop to birth." ARIZ. REV. STAT. §25–318.03.

[71] See I. Glenn Cohen & Eli Adashi, *Embryo Dispositions and Disputes: Controversies and Case Law,* 46 HASTINGS CENTER RPT. 13 (July–August 2016) (charting the cases according to jurisdiction, result and approach).

[72] See Casolo, *supra* note 66, at 321–23.

[73] Reber v. Reiss, 42 A.3d 1131 (Pa. Super. Ct. 2012); Szafranski v. Dunston, 34 N.E.3d 1132 (Ill. App. Ct. 2015). *But see* Findley v. Lee, No. FDI-13-780539 (Cal. Super. Ct. Jan. 11, 2016) (awarding embryos to ex-husband despite ex-wife's cancer treatment-induced infertility).

Legal experts encourage their clients to avoid these potential disputes by thoroughly discussing the disposition question prior to undergoing fertility treatment, and then carefully memorializing their mutually agreed-on terms in writing.[74] Medical experts implore their patients to sign pre-conception forms indicating their preferences in the event of death, divorce, failure of treatment and other possible contingencies.[75] In truth, even the most well-considered, tightly-drafted agreement cannot prevent a dispute from arising or guarantee the resolution captured writing will be enforced by a court.[76] Ultimately, the very technology that wrought this problem will solve it through advances in retrieval and cryopreservation technologies. Instead of creating embryos at the outset of treatment, parties will be increasingly encouraged to separately freeze eggs and sperm to be thawed and introduced for fertilization when the parties mutually agree they are ready for parenthood. Should a divorce intervene, each spouse walks away with control of their own gametes moving forward. As success rates for egg freezing, thawing and fertilization improve, so too will the opportunity for broader choices in assisted conception. Still, a futuristic scenario could include gametes being generated by more than one person – as is the case in MRT in which the egg houses DNA from two female sources. If two women combined to form a single egg, disputes over ultimate disposition could arise and call upon law to offer solutions.

Conclusion

A cursory review of the U.S. regulatory environment surrounding ART reveals pockets of significant and evolved state-based legal guidance amid a sparsely populated national landscape. The main role that states play in regulating the practice of medicine – reproductive and otherwise - is via a complex professional licensure and tort system. Best practices and standards of care evolve through this state-based system, admitting the possibility of variation in the practice from place to place. State courts and legislatures have been intermittently active in other areas, weighing in on the allocation of parental rights in donor gamete, surrogacy and embryo disposition scenarios. In the research arena, some states have rallied around emerging reproductive technologies as a hoped-for source of eventual biomedical and business revenues, while others have shunned any activity by banning all embryo-related research in the jurisdiction.[77] But even in the most permissive state with an

---

[74] Naomi Cahn, *Who Gets the Frozen Embryos?* FORBES (Feb. 4, 2020).

[75] *See* Practice Committee of the American Society for Reproductive Medicine, *Minimum Standards for Practices Offering Assisted Reproductive Technologies: A Committee Opinion*, 113 FERTIL. STERIL. 536 (2020).

[76] *See, e.g.,* A.Z. v. B.Z., 725 N.E.2d 1051 (Mass. 2000) (court refused to enforce agreement awarding embryos to wife as against public policy for imposing unwanted parenthood on husband).

[77] *See Ethics in Embryo Research, supra* note 29, at 276 (summarizing state laws that permit and restrict activity and funding on human embryo research).

open-arms policy toward the development of new reproductive technologies, researchers are unlikely to thrive given the limited resources states can offer in support, especially when compared to the behemoth funding structure at the national level.[78] In short, emerging technologies will struggle to find a sufficiently supportive infrastructure to develop and thrive if left to languish at the state level.

At the federal level, Congress and executive-level agencies have taken only narrow and specifically-targeted swings at ongoing clinical and research activity in the field. On the clinical side, little is demanded of ART practitioners except adherence to infection control measures and requirements to report treatment outcome data (the latter of which some in the field find onerous and selectively burdensome).[79] That said, the notion of a comprehensive top-down nationalized approach to the practice of reproductive medicine is logistically impractical, politically impossible and potentially constitutionally impermissible. The U.S. has never seriously contemplated a UK-style regulatory scheme in which individual clinics must seek permission from a centralized authority to proceed with each and every treatment cycle. Nor should it. Without a single payer healthcare system or widespread insurance reimbursement for fertility care, American patients are left to negotiate their own ART journeys through whatever means they can muster – this reality serving as the foundation for our grassroots approach to regulation. The good news is that many of the innovations that have advanced patient care have been folded into standard practice without undergoing bureaucratic holds and interminable delays. The bad news, of course, is that laissez-faire research done at the bedside without prior bench experiments, animal modeling or controlled clinical trials can produce devastating outcomes visited upon the most vulnerable in our society.

In the research realm, the federal government is the major actor because of its ability to control federal funding for emerging biologic technologies. Importantly, funding by the federal government is accompanied by a well-developed system of reporting, subject-specific oversight and institutional review of human subject research.[80] The current functional moratorium on germline gene editing and other

---

[78] The most generous state-funded program, California's Prop 71-initiatied California Institute for Regenerative Medicine (CIRM) has largely failed to produce the much-promised revenue streams. The 2004 voter ballot initiative allocated $3 billion over more than 10 years to fund stem cell therapy. A 2018 newspaper article concludes, "Not a single federally approved therapy has resulted from CIRM-funded science. The predicted financial windfall has not materialized. The bulk of CIRM grants have gone to basic research, training programs and building new laboratories, not to clinical trials testing the kinds of potential cures and therapies the billions of dollars were supposed to deliver." Eric Allday & Joaquin Palomino, *Lofty Promises, Limited Results*, SF CHRON. (Sept 6, 2018), https://projects.sfchronicle.com/2018/stem-cells/politics/

[79] In a white paper on oversight of ART issued by the American Society for Reproductive Medicine, the final sentence of the document states in bold type, "ART is already one of the most highly regulated of all medical practices in the United States." American Society for Reproductive Medicine, Oversight of Assisted Reproductive Technology (2010), https://www.asrm.org/globalassets/asrm/asrm-content/about-us/pdfs/oversiteofart.pdf

[80] *See generally* Federal Policy for the Protection of Human Subjects, 45 CFR 46, https://www.ecfr.gov/cgi-bin/retrieveECFR?gp=&SID=83cd09e1c0f5c6937cd9d7513160fc3f&pitd=20180719&n=pt45.1.46&r=PART&ty=HTML

emerging reproductive technologies precludes this robust structure from interacting with researchers at the same level of intensity and helpful redundancy that it can apply to other areas of medical research. Nearly 2 years after Dr. He Jiankui's revelation that he edited the genome of two embryos in a Chinese laboratory, only a few other reports of germline gene editing have emerged, with no other reports of live births.[81] Meanwhile, in December 2019 a Chinese court sentenced Dr. Jiankui to 3 years in prison for "illegal medical practice" in the gene editing scandal.[82] The overwhelming revulsion and punitive response to this first (mis)step on the road to germline editing will surely shape the perception and acceptability of this technology for years to come. One wonders if the same universal condemnation would have befallen a series of stepwise, assiduously monitored and verified experiments that stopped well short of implantation but yielded a trove of valuable insights into human embryology? This road not traveled is lost in the arc of science, but yields important lessons for the dangers of regulatory voids.

---

[81] See David Cyranoski, *Russian 'CRISPR-Baby' Scientist Has Started Editing Genes in Human Eggs with Goal of Altering Deaf Gene*, NATURE (Oct. 18, 2019), https://www.nature.com/articles/d41586-019-03018-0

[82] See David Cyranoski, *What CRISPR-Baby Prison Sentences Mean for Research*, SCIENTIFIC AMERICAN, (Jan. 6, 2020), https://www.scientificamerican.com/article/what-crispr-baby-prison-sentences-mean-for-research/

Part II
Cases

Transfer of Embryos Affected by Genetic Disease

Sigal Klipstein

Abstract The increasing prevalence of preimplantation genetic testing (PGT) of embryos has led to the identification of couples at risk of transmitting genetically inherited diseases to their offspring. While it is often possible to identify unaffected embryos, situations arise in which the only available embryos are ones whose transfer will certainly lead to the birth of an affected child. Such cases raise complex ethical questions, including: (1) management of situations in which one's only chance of having a genetically related child is via transfer of affected embryos, (2) the reach of physician autonomy when physicians are morally opposed to the transfer of embryos that will certainly result in affected offspring, (3) the welfare of the resultant children, (4) the permissibility of intentionally transferring an affected embryo, often to have a child who expresses the same genetics as one or both of their parents, (5) the impact of excluding affected embryos on those currently living with that particular disease given the effect such decisions might have on disability rights, (6) distributive justice concerns given that PGT is currently not available to all those who may stand to benefit due to a lack of access to care.

Keywords Preimplantation genetic testing · Affected embryo · Genetic disease · Child welfare · Disability rights

Case

A couple in their late thirties has been diagnosed with tubal infertility, necessitating in vitro fertilization (IVF). Prior to starting IVF, they undergo genetic carrier screening and discover that they are both carriers of cystic fibrosis (CF), an autosomal recessive disorder. They are counseled that they have a 25% chance of having a child affected by CF. They are given the option of testing their embryos with preimplantation genetic testing for this single gene disorder (PGT-M). They opt to do so

S. Klipstein (✉)
InVia Fertility Specialists, Chicago, IL, USA

in order to avoid the transfer of an embryo affected by CF. They undergo three IVF cycles, of which two do not produce any viable embryos. The third cycle results in three embryos that are able to be tested, and the couple is devastated to discover that all are found to be affected by CF. They ask their reproductive endocrinologist to transfer one of the affected embryos and cryopreserve the remaining two for future use. They are aware that any child resulting from these embryos would be born with CF. They express that after three IVF cycles, they lack the financial capacity and emotional strength to undergo future fertility treatments. They view the transfer of the affected embryo as their only opportunity to achieve biological parenthood and a genetic connection to their offspring.

Scope of the Question

In this scenario, the couple did not initially know that they were at risk of having a child with CF. Once they discovered this, and as they already required IVF in order to conceive, they opted to test the embryos for this disorder. Their intention was to have an unaffected child. Upon embarking on their fertility journey, they likely never considered that they would face the possibility of choosing an embryo known to carry a genetically inherited disorder. Given the new reality of their situation, they must now decide between transferring an embryo with the knowledge that the resulting child would have CF, and foregoing the opportunity to have a genetically related child.

Several questions arise. First, is it ethical to transfer an embryo when there is 100% certainty that it is affected by a disease? Does it matter that the motivation for screening embryos was to avoid transmission of this very disease? And if so, does the severity of the disease guide this decision? Should the possibility that future therapies may lessen the health burden of those with the disease factor into such decisions? What happens when conflicts occur between a patient wishing to transfer an affected embryo and a physician who believes that its transfer is unethical? How does discarding or simply not transferring affected embryos impact those who are already living with the disorder? Is there ever an argument in favor of intentionally selecting affected embryos for transfer, particularly when unaffected ones exist?

Background

Historically, genetic testing was performed for couples with a known risk of having an affected child. This could be due to an ethnicity-based risk or because of a family history of a genetically transmitted disease. Others discover that they are at risk only after the birth of a child diagnosed with an inherited disorder. A rapidly growing group of patients requesting preimplantation genetic testing include those without any known risks who are found to be carriers of a genetic disorder following screening with a preconceptual expanded carrier panel.

Preconceptual genetic testing is rapidly evolving, and embryos can be screened for virtually any disease whose genetics are known. The number of intended parents choosing to utilize this technology is rising, leading to the identification of an ever-greater number of "carrier couples." An integral part of decision making surrounding genetic testing options is genetic counseling, and the need for genetic counselors has never been greater.

Over the past decades, the genetic etiologies of thousands of diseases have been elucidated, with more being discovered on a regular basis (Genetic Alliance, OMIM). These include single gene disorders that are inherited in an autosomal dominant fashion (affecting 50% of offspring), an autosomal recessive pattern (affecting 25% of offspring) or which are X-linked (affecting 50% of male offspring).[1]

One of the goals of medicine has been to diagnose disease as early as possible in the reproductive process. Historically, diseases could only be diagnosed once symptoms developed, or pathognomonic physical characteristics were identified. Over the past half century, amniocentesis and chorionic villus sampling emerged as options to diagnose a disease prenatally. The last 30 years have opened up new technologies that allow for diagnosis of embryos prior to implantation. This ability opens the door to a number of ethical challenges.

Ethical Considerations

Patient Autonomy and the Role of the Physician

A basic tenet underlying ethical principles is a respect for patient autonomy. In the case at hand, patients have autonomy to make reproductive decisions that impact them and their future children. In the context of family building, patient autonomy is often understood as reproductive liberty. Sometimes, these decisions may be controversial. And yet, parents should be afforded great discretion in deciding the parameters under which they wish to have children.

When reproduction requires medical intervention, the physician often plays an integral role in the establishment of the pregnancy. Situations may arise in which the physician is not comfortable transferring an embryo affected by disease. Discussions regarding such potential eventualities should take place before PGT is undertaken. In other words, the possibility that only embryos affected by disease will result should be discussed with patients prior to pursuing this technology. Physicians who would not transfer embryos affected by disease should make patients aware of this

---

[1] Editor's note: see chapter "Preimplantation Genetic Testing for Adult-Onset Conditions" for more on testing for autosomal dominant, adult-onset conditions.

in advance of initiating care. This allows patients to choose a physician who will assist them should they opt to transfer an affected embryo.

Welfare of the Child

Children do not have the ability to decide whether to be born. In general, parents hope to have healthy children. Often, when children are born with a congenital anomaly or genetic disease, it was not diagnosed or predicted prior to birth. However, in the present scenario, disease is certain. A child with cystic fibrosis will likely require chronic care, have a shortened life expectancy and may also be infertile. Should the decision of whether to transfer an affected embryo hinge on known or expected disease severity? In the case of cystic fibrosis, there is a wide spectrum of disease phenotypes, ranging from a child who is mildly affected to one who is chronically ill. An additional factor to consider is the growing range of therapeutic options for those affected by cystic fibrosis. Should the hope of future treatment or cure be a determinant in whether to transfer affected embryos? Some genetically inherited diseases lead to neurological decline and certain death within the first few years of life. Such diseases include Tay Sachs and some forms of spinal muscular atrophy. Does the ethical permissibility of transferring an embryo affected by disease depend on disease severity? This should certainly be taken into account. When making decisions regarding their willingness to transfer an embryo affected by disease, physicians often balance a respect for the procreative liberty of patients with their own professional conscience. According to the Ethics Committee of the American Society for Reproductive Medicine (ASRM), "in circumstances in which a child is highly likely to be born with a life-threatening condition that causes severe and early debility with no possibility of reasonable function, it is ethically acceptable for a provider to decline a patient's request to transfer such embryos. Physician assistance in the transfer of embryos in this category is ethically problematic and therefore highly discouraged." In other circumstances, the opinion leaves the decision of whether or not to assist patients in establishing a pregnancy up to the clinician, so long as such decisions are made in an equitable manner and without bias (ASRM, 2017).

Intentional Diminishment

In the case presented at the start of this chapter, the couple elected to screen embryos with the intent of avoiding the transfer of an affected embryo. As treatment progressed, this option became unavailable. Does the fact that only affected embryos exist change this equation? How would the ethical considerations differ if they intentionally sought to create and transfer an embryo affected by disease?

A case that received significant attention two decades ago involved a same sex couple who were both deaf and hoped to conceive a deaf child. They hoped to achieve this by using a sperm donor with a five-generation family history of deafness. They felt that being deaf would be beneficial to their child, who would be able to be fully integrated into Deaf culture. They explained that as deaf parents, they could only truly understand how to raise a child who was deaf like them. According to the couple, "A hearing baby would be a blessing. A deaf baby would be a special blessing (NYT)."

This raises the concept of "intentional diminishment," in which the goal is to conceive a child who is in some way "diminished" in some characteristic, sense or health determinant (Cohen). Parents may not see the diminishment as a detrimental aspect of the child's life, but rather as a way to integrate the child into their lived reality. In some cases, it can represent an affirmation of the value of their life.

In the overwhelming majority of situations, genetic technologies are used to identify disease and disability with the goal of avoiding transmission to subsequent generations. However, requests for "intentional diminishment" occasionally arise. Such requests should be handled with compassion and an attempt to understand the motivations of the intended parents. As in the original scenario, involving embryos affected by CF, physicians will differ in their willingness to honor such requests, and should clearly express to patients whether they would be willing to participate in this type of selection scenario from the outset.

Disability Rights

When making decisions about which diseases are worthy of screening, and which embryos should not be transferred, both patients and physicians may be unwittingly making value judgments about persons affected with these diseases. While intended parents have a right to make reproductive decisions regarding preconceptual and preimplantation screening, it should be noted that these decisions may affect those already living with the disorder. If CF is often screened out, and less children with CF are born, this raises concerns that there will be less incentive to research effective drugs and treatments to help those affected by CF. There may also be less acceptance of individuals living with the disease. In families who already have one or more affected children, screening embryos to avoid having another child can lead existing children to feel less worthy or desired. It is critical that such potentialities are considered when making personal and societal decisions regarding disease screening.

Distributive Justice

While all those considering reproduction are potentially at risk for having a child affected by a genetically inherited disease, the ability to screen for these diseases in the preconceptual and preimplantation period is not evenly distributed. PGT is expensive and requires IVF. Not all those at risk of having an affected child will possess the means to benefit from this technology, or even to be screened to find out if they are at risk in the first place. This raises concerns that only the wealthy, or only those with greater access to technology, will be able to affect the disease burden on their offspring. It is imperative that society find ways to provide equitable access for disease screening to those who wish to utilize this technology.

Conclusions

The expanding ability to screen for a continually increasing number of inherited disorders prior to implantation has led to the need to consider a complex web of potential outcomes. These possibilities lead to a number of ethical considerations which must be assessed early in the decision-making process. As technology continues to increase the ability to detect genetic disorders of varying severity, nuanced decisions will be required from patients, physicians and society at large.

Works Cited/Future Readings

Handyside, A.H., Kontogianni, E.H., Hardy, K., and Winston, R.M. Pregnancies from biopsied human preimplantation embryos sexed by Y-specific DNA amplification. *Nature*. 1990; 344: 768–770

American Society for Reproductive Medicine. Use of preimplantation genetic testing for monogenic defects (PGT-M) for adult-onset conditions: an Ethics Committee opinion. *Fertil Steril*. 2018;109(6):989–992. https://doi.org/10.1016/j.fertnstert.2018.04.003

American Society for Reproductive Medicine. Transferring embryos with genetic anomalies detected in preimplantation testing: an Ethics Committee Opinion. *Fertil Steril*. 2017;107(5):1130–1135.

Daar J. A clash at the petri dish: transferring embryos with known genetic anomalies. *J Law Biosci*. 2018;5(2):219–261. Published 2018 Aug 7. https://doi.org/10.1093/jlb/lsy015

District of Columbia Department of Health. (2010). Understanding genetics: a district of Columbia guide for patients and health professionals (Appendix G, Single-Gene Disorders)

OMIM Gene Map Statistics. (2020, July 10). Retrieved January 22, 2021, from https://www.omim.org/statistics/geneMap

Cohen, I. Glenn, Intentional Diminishment, the Non-Identity Problem, and Legal Liability (January 20, 2009). Hastings Law Journal, Vol. 60, 2008.

Margarette Driscoll, Why We Chose Deafness for Our Children, SUNDAY TIMES (London), Apr. 14, 2002

Sanghavi, D. (2006). Wanting babies like themselves, some parents choose genetic defects. *The New York times on the Web*, F5–F8.

Selection to Transfer Aneuploidy/Mosaic Embryos

Kim L. Thornton

Abstract Preimplantation genetic testing for aneuploidy (PGT-A), single gene mutations (PGT-M) or structural rearrangements (SR) allows for the diagnosis of an abnormal embryo prior to embryo transfer and pregnancy. While it is not the expectation, there are instances in which prospective parents request to transfer an abnormal embryo. In the case of mosaic embryos, the embryo may implant and result in an abnormal fetus or may result in normal development. Such requests place physicians at odds with the individual or couple requesting the embryo transfer. ASRM guidelines acknowledge that arguments exist to support providers in their decision to either assist or decline transfers of abnormal embryos (Daar, J Law Biosci 5(2):219–261, 2018). Relevant ethical principles include reproductive autonomy, physician autonomy, professional conscience, nonmaleficence, procreative beneficence and child autonomy and welfare. While patients have autonomy to request transfer of aneuploidy or mosaic embryos after informed consent, physicians also have the professional autonomy to decline to proceed if they feel the outcome could result in serious disability or illness. Clinics should develop clear guidelines made available to patients and should require that genetic counselors and mental health providers are involved in the informed consent process.

Keywords Preimplantation genetic testing for aneuploidy · Preimplantation genetic testing for monogenic disease · Mosaic embryo · Reproductive autonomy · Professional conscience

K. L. Thornton (✉)
Department of Obstetrics, Gynecology and Reproductive Biology, Harvard Medical School, Boston, MA, USA

Division of Reproductive Endocrinology and Infertility, Beth Israel Deaconess Medical Center, Boston, MA, USA

Boston IVF, Waltham, MA, USA
e-mail: kthornton@bostonivf.com

© The Author(s), under exclusive license to Springer Nature Switzerland AG 2023
L. P. King, I. C. Band (eds.), *Case Studies in the Ethics of Assisted Reproduction*, https://doi.org/10.1007/978-3-031-41215-8_4

43

Case

A couple in their late thirties presents for fertility counseling after 2 years of trying to achieve pregnancy without success. Assessment revealed the female patient was affected by polycystic ovary syndrome (PCOS). Women with PCOS often experience infertility because their ovaries do not release eggs monthly, inhibiting natural conception. After several courses of ovulation-inducing drugs without pregnancy, the couple was advised to try IVF. The female patient underwent egg retrieval, and two oocytes were recovered. Given her poor response, the couple is advised to proceed with PGT-A to select the embryo with the "greatest chance of success." A full discussion of varied possible outcomes is unfortunately not undertaken. The fertilization process is successful, but PGT-A reveals that one of the embryos is chromosomally normal and one has Trisomy 21 (T21), or Down Syndrome. The couple requests that the embryo transferred be chosen at random because they feel that T21 is not incompatible with a fulfilling life.

Scope of the Question

Preimplantation genetic testing for aneuploidy (PGT-A), single gene mutations (PGT-M) or structural rearrangements (SR) has the advantage of establishing the diagnosis of an abnormal embryo prior to the establishment of a pregnancy. While in most instances, the decision to transfer only euploid or unaffected embryos is the expectation, there are instances in which the prospective parents may request to transfer an abnormal embryo affected with a disability such as congenital deafness (Lee et al., 2016) or Down Syndrome (Hens, 2015). In the case of mosaic embryos, the consideration is whether an embryo will implant and result in an abnormal fetus or whether there is a possibility that implantation and self-correction of the mosaic will result in normal development. Such a request may place physicians at odds with the couple desiring to transfer *the affected embryo*.

Background

In 2017, the American Society of Reproductive Medicine's Ethics Committee published their committee opinion on transferring embryos with genetic abnormalities detected with preimplantation genetic testing (Daar, 2018). The guideline acknowledged that "valued and reasoned arguments exist to support provider decisions to either assist …or decline to assist in such transfers." The authors cited the principles of reproductive autonomy, physician autonomy, professional conscience, nonmaleficence, procreative beneficence and child autonomy and welfare.

Ethical Considerations

Autonomy

While most patients who undergo PGT-A for aneuploidy assessment or PGT-M for single gene disorders are doing so to avoid transferring embryos with an abnormality, there are instances where a couple may request transfer of an abnormal embryo. Reasons for such a request include: (1) abnormal embryos are the only ones available and are the only option for couples to achieve biologic parenthood; (2) intended parents have a religious or other moral conviction that gives all embryos equal respect and prohibits discarding any embryos that could potentially result in life; (3) intended parents believe that some genetic diseases are still compatible with a life "worth living" and thus would not discard T21 embryos (or another variant); (4) intended parents are affected with a genetic abnormality and want to conceive children with the same disability. In the latter instance, congenital deafness and dwarfism are common examples of such a request (Baruch et al., 2006).

When patients and providers are confronted with mosaic embryos, they will consider that while most mosaic embryos do not implant or ultimately miscarry, a proportion, approximately 40%, will result in a healthy infant (Greco et al., 2015). If there is no other embryo available for transfer, couples may request, and providers may consider, transfer of mosaic embryos (Harton et al., 2017).

Intended parents may have first-hand knowledge of the disorder based on family members or children who are carriers and "affected." Arguments put forth by these intended parents tend to focus on the issue of raising children in a family of similar individuals.

Couples who undergo careful counseling and opt to proceed with transfer of embryos carrying genetic mutations are exercising their reproductive autonomy. As described in the preceding chapter, multiple stakeholders have an interest in this decision.

Providers also have autonomy to participate in or opt out of treating a patient who made such a request. Providers will consider various factors in their decision including the severity of the disorder, the age of disease onset and whether there are appropriate resources to effectively manage the disorder. Providers should discuss any potential that they would opt out of treatment ahead of testing with families.

Procreative Beneficence

The principle of procreative beneficence, first introduced in 2001 by Julian Savulescu, states that "couples should select the child, of the possible children they could have, who is expected to have the best life, or at least as good a life as the others, based on the relevant, available information" (Savulescu, 2001). Many commentators have taken issue with Savulescu's approach. A full discussion of those critiques is beyond the scope of this casebook. Persons with disabilities argue correctly that this approach devalues their existence in society if not individually. Others build upon this argument to note that our definitions of a "good life" or the "best life" are ableist and narrow. Certainly, procreative beneficence suffers greatly for lack of clarity on who and how to define what is "best."

For conditions where the result would be a severe disability or death, there is generally consensus not to transfer affected embryos. However, as described in other chapters (e.g., "Preimplantation Genetic Testing for Adult-Onset Conditions"), an embryo discarded because it carries a gene mutation cannot be said to have benefited. Putting aside arguments regarding the morality of IVF and abortion at base, and assuming for the sake of argument that existence is itself worth having, one could argue a potential child is harmed. Yet, how can we harm someone that does not exist? The non-identity problem plagues analysis here.[1] Kavka's example of the slave child and Parfit's example of the 14-year-old girl are helpful (Kavka, 1981; Parfit, 1987). In each instance, the child born although not in ideal or perhaps even desirable circumstances has no better alternative than what they in fact have been given. An embryo that has aneuploidy and the potential child that would result has no better alternative. The future advent of gene editing may change this equation.

One cannot always make a judgment as to how a child may perceive their disability in the future, however. Based on current research it is likely a child born with a disability such as Down Syndrome would view themselves as having a very full life (Friedersdorf, 2017).

Some cite legal concerns. A child that is not yet conceived cannot waive their rights to make a future claim for wrongful birth although such claims are unlikely to proceed (Ethics Committee of the ASRM, 2017). Even so, any agreement to move forward should only be done after fully informed consent, involving genetic counseling, consultation with mental health professionals and any other relevant medical specialists, is obtained (Ethics Committee of the ASRM, 2017).

When a patient requests transfer of an embryo that is mosaic, if there is a pregnancy that goes to term, the pregnancy may or may not carry the phenotype of the abnormal portion of the chromosomal abnormality. Mosaic embryos will either not implant, may implant resulting in a pregnancy with a higher miscarriage rate or may implant with risk of the child being actually aneuploid (monosomy X, trisomy 13, 14, 16, 18 and 21). In this instance, the resulting child could have disabilities that are mild, or are affected with varying degrees of severity, with some even resulting in neonatal death. In other instances, mosaicism may be confined to the placenta and result in a pregnancy with a higher rate of complications such as intrauterine growth restriction and even fetal demise (chr 2, 7, 16 and 22). Clinicians therefore have recommended a prioritized order when making the decision to transfer mosaic embryos in an effort to mitigate adverse outcomes. Embryos deemed low risk would include those mosaics with very low risk of an adverse outcome (mosaic trisomy

---

[1] Editor's note: For more information about the non-identity problem, see: Weinberg R. Existence: Who needs it? The non-identity problem and merely possible people. Bioethics. 2013 Nov;27(9):471–84.

1, 3, 10, 12 and 19). Mosaic trisomies for chromosomes 2, 5, 7 11, 17, 19 and 22 have a slightly higher risk of miscarriage and uniparental disomy (UPD). Mosaic trisomies for 6, 9 and 15 have a further increased risk of miscarriage, UPD and viable aneuploidy and should be considered with caution as do embryos with mosaic trisomy 8, 20, 47xxy or xxx. Mosaic trisomies involving 13, 14, 16, 18 and 21 and monosomy x should be avoided due to the very high risk of viable aneuploidy (Grati, 2018). Ultimately, however, patients who are well counseled should be permitted to proceed with transfer of embryos with mosaicism or genetic mutations.

Non-maleficence

As a physician, the idea of knowingly transferring an embryo that is either mosaic or is affected with a single gene disorder can be interpreted as doing harm by consciously facilitating the birth of a person that is "unhealthy" (Ethics Committee of the ASRM, 2017; Grati, 2018). Physicians are permitted when they do not agree with a parental request, to refuse to participate in their treatment but must refer to a different provider (Ethics Committee of the ASRM, 2017). The more serious the potential health implications and suffering expected for a potential child, the more ethically justifiable this refusal might be. However, providers should be encouraged to proceed whenever possible if families are well counseled and the impairment expected is non-significant. Notably in the United Kingdom, the Human Fertilization & Embryology Authority prohibits the selection of an embryo known to "have a gene, chromosome or mitochondrial abnormality involving a significant risk that [the child] will develop a serious physical or mental disability, a serious illness, or a serious medical condition." Yet, an exception is made when there is no other embryo suitable for transfer; in such cases, an anomalous embryo may be transferred. Preoperative counseling with consideration of all the potential transfer options is of paramount importance so that any differences in opinion regarding disposition of embryos may be addressed before any treatment is started.

Justice

While some make arguments that the birth of children with diseases or disabilities is harmful to society, such arguments are problematic affronts to principles of justice and nondiscrimination. In the case described above, the REI expresses concerns about the welfare of a future child with T21. However, a risk remains that a healthcare professional may falsely judge the capabilities or quality of life of the prospective child (Ethics Committee of the ASRM, 2017). In addition, if T21 is more frequently screened out and fewer children with T21 are born, there may be less acceptance of individuals living with Down Syndrome. In families where one child already has Down Syndrome, screening out embryos with T21 may make the living child feel devalued or undesired.

Conclusions

The decision to move forward with transfer of an aneuploid or mosaic embryo is a difficult one. While patients have autonomy to make the request after full informed consent, physicians also have autonomy to refuse to proceed if they feel the outcome would result in a serious physical or mental disability, a serious illness, or a serious medical condition. Development of clear guidelines or policies outlining the circumstances in which the physician will participate and the requirements for fully informed consent from genetic counselors and mental health providers are important components of care (Ethics Committee of the ASRM, 2017).

References

Baruch S, Kaufman D, Hudson KL. Genetic testing of embryos: Practices and perspectives of U.S. IVF clinics. Fertility and Sterility 2006;89(5):1053–8

Daar J. A clash at the petri dish: transferring embryos with known genetic anomalies. J Law Biosci. 2018;5(2):219–261. Published 2018 Aug 7. https://doi.org/10.1093/jlb/lsy015

Ethics Committee of the American Society for Reproductive Medicine. Transferring embryos with genetic anomalies detected in preimplantation testing: an Ethics Committee Opinion. Fertil Steril. 2017 May;107(5):1130–1135. https://doi.org/10.1016/j.fertnstert.2017.02.121. PMID: 28476180.

Friedersdorf, C. 'I Am a Man with Down Syndrome and My Life Is Worth Living'. Atlantic Monthly October 30, 2017

Grati, F. R., Gallazzi, G., Branca, L., Maggi, F., Simoni, G., & Yaron, Y. (2018). An evidence-based scoring system for prioritizing mosaic aneuploid embryos following preimplantation genetic screening. Reproductive biomedicine online, 36(4), 442–449.

Greco E, Minasi MG, Fiorentino F. Healthy Babies after Intrauterine Transfer of Mosaic Aneuploid Blastocysts. N Engl J Med. 2015 Nov 19;373(21):2089–90. https://doi.org/10.1056/NEJMc1500421. PMID: 26581010.

Harton GL, Cinnioglu C, Fiorentino F. Current experience concerning mosaic embryos diagnosed during preimplantation genetic screening. Fertil Steril. 2017 May;107(5):1113–1119. https://doi.org/10.1016/j.fertnstert.2017.03.016. Erratum in: Fertil Steril. 2017 Sep;108(3):554. PMID: 28476179.

Hens K. To transfer or not to transfer: the case of comprehensive chromosome screening of the in vitro embryo. Health Care Anal. 2015 Jun;23(2):197–206. https://doi.org/10.1007/s10728-013-0259-y. PMID: 23907565.

Kavka, G., 1981. "The Paradox of Future Individuals," Philosophy & Public Affairs, 11: 93–112.

M Lee, B Chan, P A Clark. Deafness and Prenatal Testing: A Case Study Analysis. The Internet Journal of Family Practice. 2016 Volume 14 Number 1. https://doi.org/10.5580/IJFP.39802

Parfit, 1987. Reasons and Persons, Oxford: Clarendon Press.

Savulescu J. Procreative beneficence: why we should select the best children. Bioethics. 2001 Oct;15(5–6):413–426. https://doi.org/10.1111/1467-8519.00251. PMID: 12058767.

Weinberg R. Existence: Who needs it? The non-identity problem and merely possible people. Bioethics. 2013 Nov;27(9):471–84.

Sex Selection for Nonmedical Reasons

Lacey Brennan, Isabelle C. Band, and Louise P. King

Abstract Nonmedical sex selection refers to the discretionary use of technology to fulfill the parental desire for offspring of a certain sex, rather than use of technology for the purpose of avoiding X-linked genetic conditions. The ASRM has not taken a firm position on the ethical permissibility of nonmedical sex selection but rather encourages individual clinics to develop and publicise their own policies on the subject. The autonomy of both the parents and the providers ought to be considered. Providers should consider the potential societal implications of reinforcing inaccurate gender stereotypes or the possibility of creating distorted sex ratios. As reproductive technologies continue to advance, it is essential for clinicians to carefully consider the short and long-term repercussions of using technology to select for particular traits. This chapter explores these ethical considerations with the aim of providing guidance to providers who may be faced with the decision of whether to participate in prenatal sex selection for nonmedical reasons.

Keywords Sex selection · Nonmedical sex selection · Gender stereotypes · Designer children · In vitro fertilization

L. Brennan (✉)
Division of Minimally Invasive Gynecologic Surgery, Mount Sinai Hospital, University of Toronto, Toronto, ON, Canada

I. C. Band
Icahn School of Medicine at Mount Sinai, New York, NY, USA

L. P. King
Center for Bioethics, Harvard Medical School, Boston, MA, USA

© The Author(s), under exclusive license to Springer Nature Switzerland AG 2023
L. P. King, I. C. Band (eds.), *Case Studies in the Ethics of Assisted Reproduction*, https://doi.org/10.1007/978-3-031-41215-8_5

49

Case

A 40-year-old G1P0 woman presents for fertility counseling. She and her male partner have been trying to become pregnant for the past year. They have had one 6-week spontaneous abortion and no other pregnancies. After their initial consultation, the couple decides to pursue in-vitro fertilization (IVF) and pre-implantation genetic testing for aneuploidy (PGT-A) to identify a euploid embryo and increase their chances of a successful pregnancy. The clinic proceeds with PGT-A and at the last minute the couple requests transfer of a male embryo. The couple plans to freeze remaining embryos but has no expressed plan to use them in the future.[1] The reproductive endocrinologist was not planning on participating in non-medical sex selection and is surprised by the request.

Scope of the Question

This chapter will summarize and weigh ethical issues surrounding non-medical sex selection while proposing guidelines and suggestions on how clinicians involved in assisted reproduction might respond to a scenario similar to the one described above. Although sex selection can be performed at three stages—namely, preconception, pre-implantation, or prenatal—this chapter will exclusively focus on sex selection during the pre-implantation stage. Sex selection practices can also be categorized as medical or non-medical. Sex-selection for medical reasons is generally thought to be acceptable to avoid the transmission of a sex-linked genetic disorder to the next generation (ESHRE, 2013). This chapter, instead, will focus on non-medical sex selection, which occurs in the absence of a family history of any sex-linked genetic disorder, and is viewed as a discretionary use of technology to fulfill parental desire for offspring of a certain sex.

Background

In 1999, the American Society for Reproductive Medicine (ASRM) Ethics Committee Report approved the use of preimplantation genetic diagnosis (PGD) for sex selection to avoid the birth of children at risk for sex-linked genetic disorders. The report also advised that use of PGD for sex selection when patients were already undergoing IVF for medical reasons should not be encouraged, because of risks of gender bias and social harm. In 2001, the ASRM altered their position concluding that sex selection to increase gender variety in families "may not so greatly increase

---

[1] The ethical debate is altered slightly by the intention to freeze remaining embryos rather than discarding them, as it does show some degree of intention to use non-selected embryos in the future.

the risk of harm to children, women or society that its use be prohibited or condemned as unethical in all cases" (ASRM, 2001). While the American perspective may be permissive of non-medical pre-implantation sex selection, this practice is illegal in many countries (Park et al., 2012).[2]

Fertility clinics urgently need guidance in this area where "ethical principles and legal precedents neither require nor prevent practitioners from offering these technologies to interested patients" (ASRM, 2015). The ASRM encourages clinics to develop and publicize policies of their own with regards to nonmedical sex selection, and to accommodate employee's individual opinions as to whether they wish to participate in the practice (ASRM, 2015).

In what follows, we will outline some of the most pressing ethical concerns surrounding this controversial topic and address factors that each clinic may choose to consider in crafting their own policy.

Ethical Considerations

In order to answer the important ethical questions outlined above, IVF clinics are likely to be concerned with certain key principles including autonomy, justice, nonmaleficence and a fear of creating a "slippery slope" (ESHRE, 2013). As we address the specific ethical principles at play, we will provide guidance around how to think about these principles in the context of non-medical sex selection.

Autonomy

One might ask, do patients have the right to access all of this information? Furthermore, do they have the right to act upon it? Autonomy is a highly valued principle in modern medical ethics. How far does this extend? Can we impose limitations on a patient's autonomy?

Proponents of non-medical sex selection argue that we must respect the autonomy of the prospective parents by allowing them to choose the sex of their child. Yet, the principle of autonomy also underlies the premise that clinicians and providers have the right to choose whether or not to participate in non-medical sex selection.

It may be reasonable for clinicians and providers to limit patient autonomy in select instances. When autonomy is respected without limits, medicine becomes little more than a menu for patients. It is essential for physicians not to abandon their patients in an effort to afford them "self-rule".

---

[2] Many countries, including westernized nations such as Canada, the United Kingdom, and Australia, have much stricter laws regarding pre-implantation genetic diagnosis for non-medical purposes and do not allow non-medical sex selection.

Justice

Non-medical sex selection might create a sex imbalance and reinforce patterns of sexism, especially in countries with a strong gender preference. Sex selection may contribute to social inequalities and reinforce inaccurate gender stereotypes.

Assuming a preference within a population using non-medical sex selection to select for male embryos, the repercussions of sex selection through PGS could be grave. Distorted sex ratios result in social instability, increased prostitution, trafficking and violence (Eberstadt, 2016).

Proponents of sex selection note that the risk of sex ratio distortion is only relevant to countries with strong parental preference for male children and is not a significant fear in the US (ESHRE, 2013). They also point to differences between Western and Eastern cultures related to financial burdens associated with each sex. For example, in India a daughter's dowry might bankrupt a family, while no such burden exists in the United States (King, 2007). Thus, they argue, sex selection does not carry the same risks in the U.S. as it might elsewhere.

This argument does not address concerns related to the perpetuation of erroneous gender stereotypes (discussed more fully below). Moreover, the potential exists that foreign couples could travel to the United States seeking non-medical sex selection which may result in gender inequity in their home country.

Non-maleficence

The "do no harm" principle can be applied to argue that non-medical sex selection by parents with stereotyped gender role expectations may negatively impact the welfare of the child later in life, restrict the child's development and reify gender stereotypes. Is it fair to burden the next generation by potentially increasing the pressure to conform to gender norms? Will parental expectations really be any different than those of parents who discover the sex of the fetus on ultrasound or even at birth?

A child, whose parents select their sex via non-medical sex selection may feel an undue burden to fulfill certain gender stereotypes. Parents who pursue sex selection may also be more likely to support structures that ingrain gender stereotypes and restrict other children's development (Browne, 2016). Nonmedical sex selection may also reinforce the false notion that sex and gender always align (i.e. that children are always cisgender). Presumably, relatively few parents choose their child's sex because of the genitalia that the child will have: the decision is therefore not based on biological sex but on *gender.* Parents who pursue sex selection likely assume that the child's biological sex will align with the child's gender, and that if she is born with female genitalia, she will feel like a "girl" and perform feminine roles (Browne, 2016).

Alternatively, proponents of non-medical sex selection argue that requests for sex selection do not always stem from sexist parental motivation. They point out that in some cases, sex selection can positively impact a parent-child relationship; children would not have to bear the burden of being less wanted because of their sex. Additionally, proponents of sex selection argue that parents have unrealistic expectations of their children regardless of whether or not they participate in sex selection, and that non-medical sex selection would unlikely make these expectations any more restrictive or burdensome for children. There is currently no evidence to assess the damage, or lack thereof, that might be caused by participating in sex selection and further research is warranted.

"Slippery Slope"

Concern arises that non-medical sex selection will open the door to allowing the selection of other traits, ultimately resulting in "designer children." What is the moral or practical difference between sex selection and selection of eye color, hair color or height? Where exactly should the line be drawn?

While ethicists often reject "slippery slope" arguments as conjecture, Julian Savulescu argues there is strong *pro tanto* moral obligation to select for the best child. These reasons, however, can be overcome by other considerations. Hence, he does not say that selection is what people *must* do, all things considered. Savulescu's argument here may warrant serious consideration. Once a clinic has opened its practice to providing this service, how can a clinic then limit requests for other selectable traits? From an ethical perspective, there is little argument left to limit a patient's autonomy in requesting a child with blue eyes, blond hair or greater than average height, if a clinic is willing to select for a child of a certain anticipated gender.

Of course, some ethicists would argue parents *must* actively engage in selecting the best possible children as they define it (Savulescu, 2001). These arguments were based in part on the fact that many clinics already offer non-medical sex selection. Other ethicists argue quite the opposite and note that selection of traits including sex undermines the unique and random nature of reproduction (Sandel, 2007).

Conclusions

The ASRM has not taken a firm position as to the ethical permissibility of nonmedical sex selection. Instead, the ASRM encourages individual clinics to develop and publicize their policies regarding the provision of non-medical sex selection. The ASRM also suggests that clinics accommodate employees' decisions about whether or not to participate in the practice (ASRM, 2015).

Echoing this, we recommend that clinics develop their own carefully crafted policies and include an opt out policy for REIs and embryologists who are opposed to participating in sex selection. Larger societal issues such as skewed sex ratios and entrenchment of gender stereotypes are beyond the control of individual clinics and will ultimately require oversight on a state or national level.

Clinics choosing to perform non-medical sex selection should create a policy that closely regulates the practice. Patients should be required to complete surveys and interviews to ensure that their expectations are realistic and not potentially damaging to their families, themselves or their future children. In addition, clinics should counsel patients to help mitigate any potentially negative impacts of sex selection. The ASRM ought to closely monitor, on the national level, how many patients request male versus female embryos, to ensure that there is not a significant preference for one sex or the other that may result in skewed sex ratios. Clinics who offer these services should assess the extent and profile of demand for the service. One option would be for the clinics to trial allowance of non-medical sex selection using "family balancing" as a condition for access in order to neutralize the potential dangers and disadvantages of unrestricted sex selection (ESHRE, 2013).

It is equally important for clinics choosing not to participate in sex selection to create and publicize a policy to this effect. Doing so will help to prevent and address difficult situations like the one presented in the case above and enable all parties to achieve a more desirable outcome.

Works Cited

Browne, Tamara Kayali. (2016). Parent Planning – We Shouldn't Be Allowed to Choose Our Children's Sex. *The Ethics Centre*.

Eberstadt, Nicholas. (2016). The Global War Against Baby Girls. *The New Atlantis*.

Ethics Committee of the American Society for Reproductive Medicine. (2001). "Preconception gender selection for nonmedical reasons." *Fertility and Sterility, 75(5)*, 861–864.

Ethics Committee of the American Society for Reproductive Medicine. (2015). Use of reproductive technology for sex selection for nonmedical reasons. *Fertility and Sterility, 103(6)*, 1418–1422. https://www.fertstert.org/article/S0015-0282(15)00240-X/fulltext

European Society of Human Reproduction and Embryology. (2013). ESHRE Task Force on Ethics and Law 20: sex selection for non-medical reasons. *Human Reproduction, 28(6)*, 1448–1454.

King, L. P. (2007). Clinical case: Sex selection for nonmedical reasons. *Virtual Mentor: American Medical Association Journal of Ethics, 9(6)*, 418–422.

Park, S., Bowen, W. M., & Steinbacher, R. (2012). Social and Demographic Dimensions of Sex Selection Technologies: Review and Analysis of the Research Literature. *Biodemography and Social Biology, 58(1)*, 62–74. https://doi.org/10.1080/19485565.2012.672919

Sandel, M (2007) The Case Against Perfection: Ethics in the Age of Genetic Engineering *Cambridge:Harvard University Press*

Savulescu, J (2001) Procreative Beneficience: Why We Should Select the Best Children *Bioethics* 413–426

Fertility Services for Patients with Medical Comorbidities

Isabelle C. Band and Louise P. King

Abstract Patients with underlying medical conditions are at a higher risk of peripartum complications that may compromise both their health and that of the eventual child. Reproductive autonomy is the primary consideration supporting an individual's right to access fertility treatment. However, health care providers have a duty to support the well-being of their patients and in certain cases may limit patient autonomy to prevent harm. Comorbidities may affect the health of a future child and may restrict the future parent's ability to care for the child. These concerns must in turn be balanced to avoid prioritizing ableist notions of proper parenting to determine access to fertility treatment. Reproductive endocrinologists should consult maternal fetal medicine physicians and specialists in the patient's condition to ensure that decisions regarding the provision of fertility treatment are grounded in evidence rather than stereotypes about patients with disabilities. Pregnancy remains a reasonable option for many patients with comorbidities with appropriate monitoring by subspecialists and significant counseling about risks and alternatives to pregnancy.

Keywords Comorbidities · Reproductive autonomy · Ableism · VACTERL ·
In vitro fertilization

I. C. Band (✉)
Icahn School of Medicine at Mount Sinai, New York, NY, USA

L. P. King
Center for Bioethics, Harvard Medical School, Boston, MA, USA

© The Author(s), under exclusive license to Springer Nature
Switzerland AG 2023
L. P. King, I. C. Band (eds.), *Case Studies in the Ethics of Assisted
Reproduction*, https://doi.org/10.1007/978-3-031-41215-8_6

Case

A 28-year-old G0P0 female with VACTERL association – a non-random association of congenital birth defects with findings including scoliosis, restricted lung
capacity, cardiac anomalies, limb shortening and absent thumbs – presents for fertility counseling. The patient and her male partner express wishes to have a biological
child and the patient desires to carry the pregnancy herself. Notably, the patient was
incorrectly told that VACTERL is hereditary and had a bilateral tubal ligation 8
years ago. She underwent an attempt at re-anastomosis, but success rates are low,
and she now needs IVF. Due to her scoliosis, the patient's torso is the size of an
average 11-year-old's, which might result in growth restriction of the fetus and premature delivery. Her maternal fetal medicine (MFM) specialist notes she could
likely carry a pregnancy as far as 34 weeks with some bed rest, although this is not
guaranteed. Her limb abnormalities would prohibit her from holding a child in her
arms, however her partner has no physical disabilities.

You are unsure how to proceed given the high-risk nature of the pregnancy and
the likelihood of complications for both the patient and potential fetus.

Scope of the Question

This chapter will provide an overview of the ethical issues surrounding the provision of fertility services for patients with comorbidities that may significantly
impact the health of both the pregnant person and the eventual child.

Background

In most cases, when a person gets pregnant, they remain healthy throughout their
pregnancy and give birth to a healthy infant.[1] However, complications that impact
the health of the mother and/or of the fetus can occur. In the United States, the
maternal mortality rate is approximately 24 deaths per 100,000 live births. This rate
is significantly higher for Black women and for women of advanced maternal
age [1].

There is controversy over whether IVF is associated with higher risk in pregnancy [2]. Regardless of whether a patient requires fertility treatment, patients with
underlying disease and preexisting conditions are at a higher risk of complications

---

[1] Editors' note: This chapter does not address morbidity associated with pregnancy which is near
universal and has long term effects including but not limited to changes to the pelvic floor which
result in pain and/or incontinence as well as increased risks of hypertension or diabetes for some
pregnant persons.

during pregnancy. These risks are necessarily amplified in the US where there is no universal access to preventative healthcare. Those who do not need fertility treatment typically decide whether or not to get pregnant privately [2]. In the case at hand, if the patient had not been incorrectly told that her condition was hereditary and had her tubes tied, she would have likely been able to make the decision with her partner on their own.[2] On the other hand, those who pursue fertility treatment engage in discussions about the risks of pregnancy with medical professionals. When reproductive endocrinologists (REIs) become involved in fertility treatment, it becomes less clear whether physicians can ethically offer or decline fertility treatment when the pregnancy may pose a risk to the mother or fetus [2].

Reproductive endocrinologists counsel all patients on risks associated with both fertility treatment and the pregnancy itself. Counseling of patients with comorbidities should involve MFM specialists as well as specialists in the patient's underlying disease. The counseling should occur prior to the decision of whether or not to pursue fertility treatment in order to help a patient make an informed decision [2].

Certain comorbidities, like VACTERL association, impact not only the health of the mother but potentially that of the fetus. In the case outlined above, intrauterine growth restriction (IUGR) would likely occur due to the patient's severe scoliosis and resulting small body habitus. IUGR is a common cause of perinatal mortality and morbidity. Acutely, it can result in metabolic, hematological, respiratory and thermoregulation disturbances. In addition, the patient's underlying condition would likely result in preterm birth, which is the leading cause of neonatal mortality and is associated with a host of medical problems [3]. Despite these risks to the infant, it is key to note that VACTERL association is not hereditary - therefore, the infant would not be at risk of inheriting the condition from their mother.

Ethical Considerations

Reproductive Autonomy

Reproductive autonomy, which philosopher Dworkin describes as a person's "right to control their own role in procreation unless the state has a compelling reason for denying them that control," is a value at the core of fertility treatment [4]. How far does this reproductive autonomy extend? Can we impose limitations on this autonomy when a pregnancy threatens to compromise the health of the mother or of the fetus?

The principle of reproductive autonomy is the primary consideration supporting the patient at hand's right to access fertility treatment. However, true reproductive

---

[2] Editors' note: The history of forced sterilization in the United States and elsewhere is beyond the scope of this chapter but clearly in play in this case in which a person with a disability was given incorrect information leading to their sterilization. For more information of this topic consider listening to https://radiolab.org/episodes/g-unfit

autonomy can only be achieved when the patient is informed of the risks and benefits of fertility treatment and pregnancy, and is making the decision free from undue outside pressure [2]. In addition to working with subspecialists to educate patients on the risks of fertility treatment and of pregnancy, health care professionals have an obligation to inform patients of other options including gestational surrogacy and adoption. It is also important for healthcare professionals to recognize that patients may seek out pregnancy with a genetically related child due to pressure from family members or cultural contexts. Such pressures may undermine or influence informed consent [2].

Beneficence and Non-maleficence

It is a health care professional's duty to act in the best health-related interests of patients. In some circumstances, it is reasonable for physicians to place limitations on patient autonomy to prevent harm and preserve professional integrity [5]. As such, a healthcare professional would be able to refuse to offer fertility treatment in the cases where the risks of pregnancy to the mother and fetus outweigh the potential benefit (i.e. if the risk of mortality and morbidity to the pregnant person or fetus/infant is exceptionally high). In the case at hand, the patient's pregnancy would be high-risk and could cause harm to the mother or fetus/infant. But if the patient is fully informed of the risks of pregnancy, is it always the health care professional's place to determine what is in her "best interest"?

Is it ever morally wrong to procreate? The legal term "wrongful life" – which claims that a child has to endure a not-worth-living existence – gets to the heart of this question [6]. "Procreative Beneficence," a concept coined by philosopher and bioethicist Julian Savulescu, puts forth that we have a responsibility to bear the "best possible" children [7]. In the case described above, there is a high risk of growth restriction and preterm birth, which would have repercussions on the newborn's health. These repercussions could likely be avoided if the patient were to have a child through use of a gestational surrogate. Though Savulescu makes an interesting argument about our duty to future generations, disability activists and ethicists argue that Procreative Beneficence devalues the lives of the disabled – both those conceived and in this instance those who would conceive and carry a pregnancy [8].

An additional concern in this case is that the patient's VACTERL association would negatively impact her ability to care for her future child. The healthcare professional should explore this issue with the patient, along with her partner and/or support system. Stereotypes that individuals with disabilities are less fit than others to parent are reflected in the history of eugenics, forced sterilization and in legal decisions about custody rights. Physicians must be conscious of implicit biases against parents of differing abilities, and recognize that parenting can occur in different ways [9]. The Americans with Disabilities Act of 1990, "which applies to private fertility clinics, prohibits denying persons with disabilities access to infertility services if the denial is based on ill-founded doubts or stereotypes about their ability to rear and parent [10]." As noted in the case, the patient's partner is also eager to have a child, has no physical disabilities, and plans to work with the patient to raise the future child.

Sister Song Collective defines reproductive justice as "the human right to maintain personal bodily autonomy, have children, not have children, and parent the children we have in safe and sustainable communities [11]." Within this intersectional framework that encompasses race, class, gender and *ability*, it is critical to create space for a feminist movement that emphasizes choice for all bodies, not just mainstream ones (see more complete discussion of Reproductive Justice in Section "Framework for Analysis") [12].

Justice

Health care professionals vary in terms of the amount of risk they are willing to take on in caring for their patients [2]. At times, their decisions to offer or not to offer reproductive health care may be informed by ableist bias. To counter this potential and ensure justice is maintained, the reproductive endocrinologist should consult a VACTERL association specialist, an MFM health care professional, and clinical/ethical guidelines to help determine the level of risk the patient would face in undergoing fertility treatment and pregnancy. This would allow the REI specialist to make a decision about whether or not to offer fertility services based on facts rather than on biases or discrimination. If an REI specialist goes through these necessary steps and still feels that the potential harm of offering treatment would outweigh the benefits, it would be reasonable for an REI specialist to decline to proceed and to refer the patient to a colleague if possible.

Conclusion

For most patients, even those with significant comorbidities, pregnancy remains a reasonable option with appropriate monitoring by subspecialists in MFM and in the patient's particular underlying disease [2]. In determining whether to offer or decline fertility treatment to patients with significant comorbidities while adhering to ethical principles, physicians should:

- Counsel the patient on the risks associated with fertility treatment and pregnancy
- Review alternatives to fertility treatment and pregnancy, including gestational surrogacy and adoption
- Consult with subspecialists in MFM and in the patient's specific underlying condition
- Review existing clinical and ethical guidelines

- Consider seeking out a second opinion
- Make reasonable efforts to ensure that the patient is not being pressured into pursuing pregnancy by family members or cultural context [2]
- Ensure that when care is declined, it is due to medical facts, in consultation with specialists and without discrimination

Works Cited

1. Maternal Mortality Rates in the United States, 2020. Published February 22, 2022. Accessed June 29, 2022. https://www.cdc.gov/nchs/data/hestat/maternal-mortality/2020/maternal-mortality-rates-2020.htm
2. Provision of fertility services for women at increased risk of complications during fertility treatment or pregnancy: an Ethics Committee opinion. *Fertil Steril.* 2022;117(4):713–719. https://doi.org/10.1016/j.fertnstert.2021.12.030
3. Prematurity: Practice Essentials, Background, Pathophysiology. Published online March 15, 2022. Accessed June 29, 2022. https://emedicine.medscape.com/article/975909-overview
4. Dworkin R. *Life's Dominion.* Harper Collins; 1993.
5. Brennan L, King L. Transferring Genetically Affected Embryos in IVF. Accessed June 29, 2022. https://bioethics.hms.harvard.edu/journal/ivf-affected-embryos
6. Frati P, Fineschi V, Di Sanzo M, et al. Preimplantation and prenatal diagnosis, wrongful birth and wrongful life: a global view of bioethical and legal controversies. *Hum Reprod Update.* 2017;23(3):338–357. https://doi.org/10.1093/humupd/dmx002
7. Savulescu J. Procreative beneficence: why we should select the best children. *Bioethics.* 2001;15(5–6):413–426. https://doi.org/10.1111/1467-8519.00251
8. Wasserman D. The Nonidentity Problem, Disability, and the Role Morality of Prospective Parents. *Ethics.* 2005;116(1):132–152. https://doi.org/10.1086/454369
9. Cureton A. Parents with Disabilities. The Oxford Handbook of Reproductive Ethics. https://doi.org/10.1093/oxfordhb/9780199981878.013.19
10. Child-rearing ability and the provision of fertility services: a committee opinion. *Fertil Steril.* 2013;100(1):50–53. https://doi.org/10.1016/j.fertnstert.2013.02.023
11. Reproductive Justice. Sister Song. Accessed July 14, 2022. https://www.sistersong.net/reproductive-justice
12. Sterilization of People With Disabilities: Acknowledging the Past and Present History, Rhetoric, and Effects of a Harmful Practice – RightsViews. Published January 27, 2019. Accessed April 9, 2023. https://blogs.cuit.columbia.edu/rightsviews/2019/01/27/sterilization-of-people-with-disabilities-acknowledging-the-past-and-present-history-rhetoric-and-effects-of-a-harmful-practice/

Preimplantation Genetic Testing for Adult-Onset Conditions

Avner Hershlag

Abstract Preimplantation genetic testing for monogenic disease (PGT-M) can detect both childhood and adult-onset diseases. Unlike most childhood-onset genetic disorders, adult-onset conditions are typically dominant (presenting in 50% of offspring) and are associated with disease-free life until some point in adulthood. Examples discussed include BRCA mutation-associated cancers and Huntington's disease. Ethical questions explored include: (1) the implications on a patient's own moral value when they use PGT-M to rid a future child of a trait they possess, (2) exercising reproductive autonomy to undergo PGT-M, and to select an affected (or unaffected) embryo balanced against professional autonomy and procreative beneficence, (3) timing for information-sharing with future children, (4) the potential that an embryo biopsy may harm the embryo or pregnant person, (5) a duty to maximize benefit and minimize harm to a future child and (6) justice issues given the high cost of PGT-M and the fact that it is frequently not covered by insurance. Patients should receive extensive counseling by genetic counsellors and physicians that involves the exploration of testing options other than PGT-M. The ASRM Ethics Committee considers PGT-M for adult-onset disease ethically justifiable when there are no known interventions for the disease or when the available interventions are ineffective or significantly burdensome (Fert Steril 109:989–992 2018). Physicians may decline to transfer embryos that carry genetic mutations but should share this position with the patient(s) in a pre-IVF consult and should remain open to referring to other qualified providers in order to preserve patient autonomy.

Keywords Preimplantation genetic testing for monogenic disease · Adult-onset disease · Huntington's disease · BRCA · Moral value

A. Hershlag (✉)
Department of Obstetrics, Gynecology and Reproductive Medicine, Renaissance School of Medicine, Stony Brook University, Stony Brook, NY, USA

Department of Obstetrics, Gynecology and Reproductive Medicine, Donald and Barbara Zucker School of Medicine at Hofstra/Northwell, Hempstead, NY, USA

Island Fertility, University Associates in Obstetrics and Gynecology, Commack, NY, USA

© The Author(s), under exclusive license to Springer Nature Switzerland AG 2023
L. P. King, I. C. Band (eds.), *Case Studies in the Ethics of Assisted Reproduction*, https://doi.org/10.1007/978-3-031-41215-8_7

Case 1a: BRCA-1 Mutation Carrier

A 40-year-old woman, never pregnant, is desirous of conception. Her husband has abnormal sperm parameters. At the age of 31 she had a bilateral mastectomy for breast cancer with reconstruction followed by tamoxifen. She was found to be a carrier of a BRCA-1 mutation. Her father, Ashkenazi Jewish, had passed from pancreatic cancer at age 50. His sister was diagnosed with breast cancer at 32, recurrent at 34, which she had survived, but then developed ovarian cancer at age 65 as well as melanoma. She died with pulmonary hypertension, 80-years-old. The paternal grandfather died at age 70 with lymphoma. The patient desired IVF, agreed to PGT-A, but only reluctantly to PGT-M for the BRCA-1 gene.

An IVF cycle yielded three blastocysts that could be biopsied. Three were euploid, but only one was a euploid male negative for the BRCA-1 mutation. This embryo was transferred, and the patient delivered a healthy boy.

Scope of the Question

This chapter will address the ethical issues involving diagnosis of adult (late-onset) genetic disease in embryos, through PGT-M (preimplantation genetic testing for monogenic disease, previously named PGD). Several distinctions set adult-onset genetic diseases apart from conditions presenting at infancy and childhood, most notably the possibility of a disease-free life until some point in adulthood. Most adult-onset conditions are dominant, presenting in 50% of embryos/offspring that carry them. Childhood-onset genetic disorders, on the other hand, are almost always recessive, with a 25% chance of an affected embryo/child. When prospective parents seek PGT-M for a recessive condition that presents in childhood, they are typically carriers and do not have the condition themselves. On the other hand, with dominant late-onset conditions, one of the parents usually carries the mutation themselves. Adult-onset genes vary in penetrance. Cancer gene mutations present an additional ethical challenge as not all carriers will develop cancer.

Background

Some of the unique aspects of adult-onset conditions are addressed in the ASRM Ethics Committee Opinion (2018). The committee states that, "—PGT-M for adult-onset disease is ethically justifiable when the conditions are serious and when there are no known interventions for the conditions, or the available interventions are either inadequately effective or perceived to be significantly burdensome." Mutations in the BRCA-1 gene fall into the latter category. "Effective intervention" is possible through proactive surgical prophylaxis or cancer treatment as indicated. Bilateral risk-reducing mastectomy (BRRM) reduces the occurrence of breast cancer, in some series to 0%, while impact on long-term survival has not been shown (Carbine, 2018). Risk-reducing salpingo-oophorectomy (RRS) decreases the risk of ovarian and fallopian tube cancer by 80–90% (ACOG Bulletin, 2017).

Ethical Considerations

Autonomy

This patient was aware that she carried a BRCA-1 mutation. She was a breast cancer survivor after bilateral mastectomy and thus fully aware of what a child with the mutation could face later in life. Yet she was reluctant to have her embryos tested for the gene mutation. Why? In practice, we find that this is not an uncommon reaction by patients with adult-onset disease. The proposed goal is to eliminate embryos that carry the BRCA-1 variant. As she carries the gene, she may either consciously or unconsciously question her own "value" or moral status when confronted with this decision. Is her own life being devalued by choosing to rid her offspring of a gene she herself carries? (President's Council on Bioethics, 2017).

Genetic counseling ahead of testing is strongly recommended (ASRM Ethics Committee 2018). Alternatives to PGT-M should be discussed, including proceeding without any testing or prenatal diagnosis during pregnancy by chorionic villus sampling (CVS) or amniocentesis and in the future by non-invasive prenatal diagnosis (NIPD). Patients may choose those options to know if the fetus is carrying the gene or to inform decisions about termination. Notably prenatal diagnosis does not commit the patient to terminate an affected pregnancy, although that is the most common consequence of a positive test.

Following non-directive genetic counseling, the patient decided to have her embryos screened for the BRCA-1 gene variant, in addition to chromosomal screening. Whatever this patient's decision regarding testing, reproductive endocrinologists are encouraged to proceed out of respect for the patient's reproductive autonomy. A similar argument can be made should this patient at a later date ask for transfer of an embryo carrying the BRCA gene. However, physicians also arguably have the ability to autonomously refuse to proceed with this transfer. If a practice anticipates that they will be unwilling to transfer an embryo with any particular genetic trait they should make the patient aware of this ahead of proceeding with testing.

By contrast, a child born with a BRCA diagnosis has arguably lost some level of autonomous decision making. While adult patients are given the option in non-directive genetic counseling to forgo knowing their genetic predispositions to disease, a child born with this diagnosis presents a conundrum in terms of future counseling. At what point should families discuss this diagnosis if at all with children? As this is an adult-onset disease, should it be discussed only when the person reaches adulthood? Likely these determinations would be made on a case-by-case basis but should be delayed until adulthood if possible. Parents should be aware of complicating factors when deciding about testing whether pre-implantation or pre-natal.

Beneficence/Non-maleficence

At the outset, there is no current evidence that embryo biopsy has a negative impact on the embryo (reviewed by Cimadomo et al. 2020). Biopsy does increase risk to the mother as it may increase the risk of monozygotic twinning: 2.4% versus 1.5% following non-PGT IVF, according to a recent large British study (Kamath et al. 2020). The risk of a misdiagnosis as a result of Allele Dropout (ADO) has been practically eliminated by the most recent PGT-M techniques of genome-wide SNP array or next generation sequencing (NGS)-based haplotyping techniques (ESHRE PGT 2020). However, other errors and risks are still possible, including compromised DNA integrity due to biopsy technique, inconclusive or false results due to suboptimal laboratory conditions, or test failure due to insufficient markers or other technical reasons and errors in sample tracking (ESHRE PGT 2020).

An embryo discarded because it carries the BRCA gene variant cannot be said to have benefitted from this process. Given the non-identity problem, as described in the chapter "Selection to Transfer Aneuploidy/Mosaic Embryos," an embryo carrying the BRCA variant and the potential child that would result has no more desirable alternative. Future advancement of gene editing may change this. A child born without a pathogenic BRCA variant has clearly benefited from testing as their chance to undergo extirpative surgery, intense surveillance and potentially cancer treatment is dramatically reduced to that of the general population. The chance of breast cancer in a BRCA-1 variant carrier male is 1.2% (versus 0.1% in the general population); for prostate cancer 8.6% by age 65 (vs. 6%) and for pancreatic cancer 1–3% (vs. 0.5%) (Ibrahim et al. 2018; Dullens et al. 2020). In a female, the cumulative breast cancer risk up to age 80 was 72% (versus 13% in the general population); a second cancer in the contralateral breast 40% within 20 years. The cumulative ovarian cancer risk up to age 80 was 44% (versus 1–2% in the general population) (Kuchenbaecker et al. 2017; Dullens et al. 2020). A family may feel stress and guilt, knowing that their child has a 50% chance of having a cancer-mutated gene (and according to the American Academy of Pediatrics – testing is not recommended until the child turns 18 years old) (American Academy of Pediatrics, 2013). Transferring only embryos that do not carry the BRCA variant will stop its transmission to the offspring and future generations to come.

Justice

Access to care is the major issue relating to fairness in providing a rather sophisticated and expensive procedure. In the case presented, the patient had already requested IVF and embryo biopsy to test for chromosomal aneuploidy (PGT-A), so the only added expense is the PGT-M itself (Ethics Committee of the American Society for Reproductive Medicine 2021).

Only 24% of Americans have access to Assisted Reproductive Technologies and even those who have access frequently find that PGT-M is not covered by insurance. While the BRCA gene variants do not discriminate between different socio-economic classes, the present health system in America does, thus leaving lower classes at a disadvantage in securing the health of their future children. Some patients are reluctant to request PGT-M for fear of their premium increasing and/or the breach of confidentiality. Even the initial testing for cancer-causing genetic variants may not be covered.

A recent study found that PGT-M for BRCA-1 and 2 is cost-effective at an assumed pay of $50,000 per quality-adjusted life-year (QALY) (Lipton et al. 2020). However, this study assumed a single payer system of healthcare. The cost of testing in the US is typically borne by the parents-to-be, whereas the cost of treatment if any is borne by one of many insurers. Without a single payer system, this cost analysis is inapplicable to the situation in the US.

Patients' literacy level affects their comprehension of the procedure and its potential benefits. A recent study concluded that educational materials about IVF+PGT-M are not "readable, understandable, or clear" (Early et al. 2020). The materials did not meet the CDC requirement of a 90% comprehensibility nor the Joint Commission requirement that education materials should be at or below 5th grade level. This recent work points to, a probably unintended, literacy discrimination.

In short, the US health care system is not in a position to ensure that justice exists regarding PGT- M for any disorder nor gene editing in the future. Without addressing these disparities, the practice on a societal level may be unethical.

Case 1b: BRCA1 Mutation Carrier

The patient returned, now 41, desirous of another child. She had only two embryos remaining, a male and a female, both carrying her BRCA-1 mutation. After non-directive genetic counseling she opted to transfer the female mutated BRCA-1 embryo to "balance" her family as her first child is male (see discussion of family "balancing" in the chapter "Sex Selection for Nonmedical Reasons").

The patient's options included another IVF-PGT-M cycle, transfer of an affected male embryo, given lower risk or transfer of the affected female embryo. After the non-directive genetic counseling, she determined that her goals for family balancing outweighed any risks she saw for a future female child carrying the same pathogenic BRCA variant that she carries.

In her decision to have an affected female embryo transferred, the patient is exercising one of the fundamental cornerstones of medical ethics: reproductive autonomy. Yet, some ethicists may disagree and cite the principle of "Procreative Beneficence," noting that this patient has the option of selecting a male embryo with less potential lifetime risk. A variety of considerations then come into play, not least of which as described above is the inherent message the patient herself might consciously or subconsciously receive from this directive regarding her own value. The ASRM Ethics Committee has resolved these complex conflicts of ethical principles by noting that physicians may decline to proceed with transfer of embryos known to carry genetic mutations. Ideally, if this outcome is seen as a potential, reproductive endocrinologists should discuss with patients in the pre-IVF with PGT-M consult their position regarding the transfer of an affected embryo. Should the physician (exercising her or his Physician Autonomy) not intend to transfer a genetically affected embryo under any circumstances, the patients, should they desire to keep that option open (Patient Autonomy), should be advised (and even referred) to seek care elsewhere.

Case 2: Huntington's

A 33-year-old woman, married for 6 years, never pregnant, presented to my office shortly after her father passed away at age 64 from Huntington's disease (HD). Neither the patient nor her sister have been tested for HD. It has been presumed, though not proven by testing, that three ancestral family members could have possibly been affected by HD: paternal grandmother, paternal great aunt, and paternal great grandfather. The patient and husband request IVF with PGT-M to ascertain that their child will not inherit the Huntington Disease gene variant. However, the patient does not want to find out if she is a carrier of her father's lethal variant.[1]

Background

Huntington's disease (HD) is an autosomal dominant adult-onset neurodegenerative disease. It is caused by an abnormal expansion of the CAG repeats in the gene for the Huntingtin protein on chromosome 4 (Pandey and Rajamma 2018). There seems to be an inverse relationship between the number of CAG repeats and the age of onset of HD (Tabrizi et al. 2013). For example: age of onset of HD with 41 repeats is over 50, 45 repeats less than 40, and 50 repeats less than 30 years of age. Psychiatric symptoms are usually first to appear (depression, anxiety and sleep

---

[1] Editors' note: for further discussion of a similar case see https://pubmed.ncbi.nlm.nih.gov/28813239/

disorders), then motor abnormalities (chorea, dyskinesia, dystonia) and cognitive decline (defocused, difficulty with new information retention, language decline, disorganized speech, abnormal perception). Ultimately, HD progresses to motor rigidity and dementia and is fatal (Pandey and Rajamma 2018).

After experiencing the downhill spiral her father went through, the patient is faced with several choices, none of them easy. She and her husband have had extensive genetic counseling. She knows she has a 50% chance of carrying the genetic variant. Does she want to know? Depression and suicide have been observed in patients who knew they had HD, all of them having suffered through a dreadful rehearsal watching their parent's progressive deteriorations and ultimate deaths. This patient did not want to know if she carries the gene. Her options include not having children, having biological children with a possible 50% chance of carrying the gene, if she was a carrier, or undergoing IVF with PGT-M, in which instance three choices remain:

"Standard PGT-M"

Prior to testing the embryos, the PGT lab will test the patient (and her husband as a control). Therefore, the patient will know if she carries the mutated gene or not. If she is not a carrier, she doesn't need to proceed with PGT-M.

With the potential diagnosis of having the HD gene, the patient faces not only the psychological impact that comes with knowing you will die at a young age, but also the worry about a potential breach of confidentiality that could affect her employability, health insurance, life insurance and many other aspects of her life.

Some protection may be afforded by the GINA (Genetic Information and Nondiscrimination Act) Law signed in 2008. It is governed by the US Equal Employment Opportunity Commission. Once the disease manifests itself, however, GINA no longer applies (though other laws, such as the Americans with Disabilities Act might provide some protection) (Green et al. 2015a, b).

Since 2014, the Affordable Care Act (ACA) prohibits refusal of coverage or changing insurance rates based on pre-existing conditions. The only exception is "grandfathered" health plans. However, as with any law, this is subject to change.

Non-disclosure

This is one of two ways the patient can request PGT-M for her embryos, while she remains oblivious to whether she carries the gene variant or not. Both parents are tested for the gene. However, the parents and clinical staff are unaware of the genetic status of the parents (Asscher and Koops 2010a, b). Keeping the staff blinded may prove logistically challenging.

Patients may choose the non-disclosure option for a variety of reasons including: their autonomous right not to know; fear of discrimination despite GINA and the ACA; avoiding the stigma of a fatal diagnosis; reducing anxiety and depression; and avoiding any impact on personal relationships (McCusker and Loy 2017a, b).

Exclusion Testing

"Exclusion testing" minimizes the possibility of inheriting the mutation by selecting against chromosome number 4 of the affected grandparent. All embryos that might be affected are excluded. The advantage is that the patient's genetic status remains unknown without a need to blind the staff (Asscher and Koops 2010a, b). However, if the patient is not affected (which will occur in half of the cases), embryos have been excluded unnecessarily.

Conclusion

Each of the three options above will afford the benefit of respecting a patient's autonomous choices not only regarding her reproduction but also regarding her knowledge of her disease carrier state. Extensive counseling by the physician and genetic counselors is crucial to guide the patient through this complex decision-making process.

At present, the option of non-disclosure seems to be the least favored, since the lack of transparency, even per her request, may not sit well with physicians and genetic counselors alike. This leaves us with the two other options: if the patient is willing to be tested, the PGT-M process will follow like any other genetic testing of embryos. If the patient doesn't want to know if she carries the HD gene, the exclusion testing will keep that information veiled for the patient and the medical team alike.

Works Cited/Further Reading

Ethics Committee of the American Society for Reproductive Medicine. (2018) "Use of Preimplantation genetic testing for monogenic defects (PGT-M) for adult-onset conditions." *Fertility and Sterility, 109:989–92.*

Ethics Committee of the American Society for Reproductive Medicine. Electronic address: asrm@asrm.org. Disparities in access to effective treatment for infertility in the United States: an Ethics Committee opinion. Fertil Steril 2021; 116(1):54–63. https://doi.org/10.1016/j.fertnstert.2021.02.019

Carbine et al, Cochrane Database Syst Rev 2018; 4: CD002748. https://www.cochranelibrary.com/cdsr/doi/10.1002/14651858.CD002748.pub4/full

Hereditary Breast and ovarian Cancer syndrome. ACOG Practice Bulletin No. 182. American College of Obstetricians and Gynecologists. Obstetrics Gynecol 2017; 130:e110–26 https://www.acog.org/clinical/clinical-guidance/practice-bulletin/articles/2017/09/hereditary-breast-and-ovarian-cancer-syndrome

American Academy of Pediatrics, Committee on Bioethics, Committee on Genetics, and American College of Medical Genetics and Genomics Social, Ethical and Legal Issues Committee Ethical and policy issues in genetic testing and screening of children. Pediatrics 2013;131:620–2.

Ibrahim M, Yadac S, Ogunleye F, Zakalik D. Male BRCA mutation carriers: Clinical characteristics and cancer spectrum. (2018); BMC Cancer 18:179

President's Council on Bioethics, Eugenics and Inequality. Reproduction and responsibility: the regulation of new biotechnologies. Available at: https://bioethicsarchive.georgetown.edu/pcbe/reports/reproductionandresponsibility/chapter1.html Last accessed August 15, 2017.

Lipton JH et al, Cost effectiveness of in vitro fertilization and preimplantation genetic testing to prevent transmission of BRCA1/2 mutations. 2020. Human Reproduction 35(2):434–445.

Green RC et al. N Engl J Med 2015a; 372:397–399

McCusker EA and Loy CT. Tremor other Hyperkinet Mov 2017a:7:467

Asscher E, Koops BJ. J Med Ethics 2010a; 36:30–33

Kuchenbaecker KB et al. Risks of breast, Ovarian and contralateral breast cancer for BRCA1 and BRCA2 mutation carriers. JAMA 2017; 317(23):2402–2416

Dullens et al. Cancer surveillance in healthy carriers of germline pathogenic variants in BRCA1/2: A review of secondary prevention guidelines. 2020. J Oncol published online June 2020 https://doi.org/10.1155/2020/9873954

Kamath MS et al. Zygotic splitting following embryo biopsy: a cohort study of 207, 697 single-embryo transfers following IVF treatment. BJOG 2020;127(5):562–569

Cimadomo D, Rienzi L, Capalbo A, Rubio C, Innocenti F, García-Pascual CM, Ubaldi FM, Handyside A. The Dawn of the future: 30 years from the first biopsy of a human embryo. The detailed history of an ongoing revolution. Hum Reprod Update. 2020 Jun 18;26(4):453–473.

ESHRE PGT-M Working Group, Carvalho F, Moutou C, Dimitriadou E, Dreesen J, Giménez C, Goossens V, Kakourou G, Vermeulen N, Zuccarello D, De Rycke M. ESHRE PGT Consortium good practice recommendation for the detection of monogenic disorders. Hum Reprod Open. 2020 May 29;2020 https://doi.org/10.1093/hropen/hoaa018

Early ML, Kumar P, Marcell AV, Lawson C, Christianson M, Pecker LH. Literacy assessment of preimplantation genetic patient education materials exceed national reading level. J Assist Reprod Genet 2020 May 29 online https://doi.org/10.1007/s10815-020-01837-z

Pandey M, Rajamma U. Huntington's Disease: the coming of age. J of Genetics 2018;97(3):649–664

Tabrizi S. J., Scahill R. I., Owen G., Durr A., Leavitt B. R., Roos R. A. *et al.* 2013 Predictors of phenotypic progression and dis- ease onset in premanifest and early-stage Huntington's disease in the TRACK-HD study: analysis of 36-month observational data. *Lancet Neurol.* **12**, 637–649.

Green RC et al. N Engl J Med 2015b; 372:397–399

McCusker EA and Loy CT. Tremor other Hyperkinet Mov 2017b:7:467

Asscher E, Koops BJ. J Med Ethics 2010b; 36:30–33

Fertility Services for Patients of Advanced Reproductive Age

Dale W. Stovall

Abstract Requests to proceed with assisted reproduction at advanced ages require careful consideration of risks balanced against ethical concerns. Key ethical issues include: (1) Patient autonomy to determine whether and when to become a parent, assuming that the patient is educated about all medically acceptable options, (2) health care provider/ART clinic autonomy to develop fact-based guidelines that limit a patient's reproductive options regarding age, (3) physician duty to promote wellbeing (beneficence) and prevent harm (non-maleficence) to a patient, fetus or neonate, and (4) acknowledgment that assisted reproduction is a scarce resource to which few individuals have access and that pregnancy at an advanced age likely requires a higher level of care. To promote justice, reproductive health care professionals should work to ensure an equitable distribution of resources while being aware of how ageism may shape the plans they propose to patients.

Keywords Advanced reproductive age · Justice · Ageism · Autonomy · Non-maleficence

Case

A 52-year-old woman and her male partner present to a reproductive endocrinologist for counseling. She expresses that she has always wanted children but her intense career as a litigator has always interfered. She has never been pregnant. Now, at 52, she and her husband want to have a child. She has undergone menopause and realizes that she cannot have a child genetically related to herself, but she is willing to use a donor egg and her husband's sperm to carry the child to term.

D. W. Stovall (✉)
Department of Obstetrics & Gynecology, Texas Christian University Burnett School of Medicine, Methodist Health System – Dallas, Dallas, TX, USA

© The Author(s), under exclusive license to Springer Nature Switzerland AG 2023
L. P. King, I. C. Band (eds.), *Case Studies in the Ethics of Assisted Reproduction*, https://doi.org/10.1007/978-3-031-41215-8_8

71

Scope of the Question

This chapter will provide a summary of the ethical considerations surrounding the provision of fertility services to patients of advanced reproductive age.

Background

Oocyte and embryo donation are both accepted and successful assisted reproductive technologies (ART), and their use has continued to increase in the United States [1, 2]. These techniques help both individual patients and couples, who would otherwise not be able to conceive, to start a family. The US Food and Drug Administration (FDA), US Centers for Disease Control and Prevention (CDC), American Association of Tissue Banks (AATB), and the American Society for Reproductive Medicine (ASRM) have all produced guidelines in regard to oocyte and embryo donation. These documents cover issues such as donor and recipient eligibility, a variety of donor screening issues, and laboratory testing.

Successful oocyte donation and subsequent pregnancy has been reported in women in their 50s and early 60s [3, 4]. These reports demonstrate the ability of oocyte donation to extend a woman's reproductive abilities into the years after menopause. However, unlike the use of oocyte or embryo donation to "treat" pathological conditions which result in premature ovarian insufficiency, using these technologies to extend reproduction past one's "natural" reproductive years challenges our understanding of the purpose of reproductive medicine.

In 2013, the Ethics Committee of the ASRM published its first manuscript regarding oocyte or embryo donation to women of advanced reproductive age (ARA). A revised committee opinion on this subject was published in 2016 [5]. Key points of the later document included the fact that although oocyte donation reverses the age-related decline in implantation and birth rates of women in their 40s and 50s, both maternal and neonatal risks associated with this procedure are higher and need to be carefully considered. Therefore, before proceeding with embryo transfer for a woman of ARA, both a medical and psycho-social evaluation of the patient or couple should be performed.

Ethical Considerations

Autonomy
Clinicians understand the need to respect the medical decisions made by other people concerning their own health and lives. Not only does this concept define the principle of autonomy, but it also defines the principle of basic human dignity. Patient choice and patient involvement are paramount in both the treatment

decision-making process and in the success of the treatment plan itself. Before consenting to a treatment option, however, patients need to be fully informed regarding all medically acceptable options. This process allows for proper consent to treatment and an individualized treatment plan as opposed to a "one size fits all" methodology.

Support for oocyte donation for a couple or individual of ARA is similar to that for a couple or individual of "reproductive age". The concept for both is that every individual should have the ability to decide whether or not to become a parent, and just as important, when in their lives that they are the most prepared to be a parent.

However, autonomy is important in regard to both the patient and the health care professional. In this regard, either an individual health care professional or an ART program may have their own policy or guidelines that limit a patient's reproductive autonomy in regard to their age and the performance of various reproductive services. It is important in this instance for healthcare professionals and ART programs alike, to develop factually based guidelines and to be aware of how one's personal and professional values may impact these decisions.

Beneficence

It is important to all health care professionals to continually promote the well-being of others through their actions and to perform procedures that provide benefits and that prevent harm. We want our services to not only be helpful, but to be of high clinical quality and value. It is for this reason that healthcare professionals constantly evaluate the processes involved in their ART and other infertility services, strive for continued improvement in all important clinical outcomes, and adhere to the National minimum standards of practice.

Oocyte donation is now an established standard of practice for the treatment of age-related infertility and is associated with high rates of pregnancy success with live birth rates per embryo transfer above 50% [6]. For this couple, it seems reasonable to conclude that if all goes well and the oocyte donation procedure results in a healthy infant, that this result will have a significant positive impact.

In the US and throughout the world it is not uncommon for children to be partially or completely raised by their grandparents. Although this practice may be out of necessity, it does help to demonstrate that parents of ARA can have both the physical and psychological abilities to successfully parent. Limiting access to assisted reproduction on the basis of advanced age alone does not comport and is likely too restrictive. In other guidance, the ASRM cautions against arbitrary denials of care unless the safety of future children is demonstrably threatened [7].

Non-maleficence

In addition to promoting well-being, it is also the obligation of the clinician to avoid inflicting harm to others. Clinicians should not encourage the participation of their patients in procedural therapies or other interventions that could result in significant harm. In this case, it is important to consider the adverse impact that the lack of success in regard to a live birth or complications that may arise in pregnancy, delivery, or postpartum may have.

As in a patient of any age who is considering an ART procedure, a routine health and reproductive history should be obtained that is within the standards that are applied to individuals anticipating pregnancy. The goal of pre-pregnancy care is to reduce the risk of adverse health effects for the woman,[1] fetus, and neonate by working with the woman to optimize health, address modifiable risk factors, and provide education [8]. Pre-pregnancy care should include but is not limited to the following: review of all medications, assessment of exposure to teratogens, a psychiatric history, a substance use and abuse history, a family and genetics history, assessment of exposure to violence, assessment of immunization and nutritional status, a surgical history, assessment of physical activity, and maternal weight issues. Other tests that are recommended to optimize perinatal care include assessment of Rh factor and infectious disease testing.

To assist with the complex psycho-social aspects associated with having a child through oocyte donation and to reduce harm in this regard, a psycho-educational consultation with a licensed mental-health professional who has training in third-party reproduction should be performed. During the consultation, the couple should be educated regarding the emotional and social implications concerning having a child through oocyte donation, and a determination should be made if adequate supports are in place to raise a child to adulthood given the advanced age of the parents. This consultation will help the couple make informed decisions regarding disclosure of oocyte donation to their offspring, the needs of donor-conceived persons including implications of having persons who are linked through the same donor, grief associated with treatment failure or ART cycle cancellation, transition to parenthood, and more specifically parenting at an older age.

It is well documented that the pregnancies of women who undergo oocyte donation over age 50 are associated with increased risks during gestation, labor, and at the time of delivery. Specific risks include an increased rate of operative delivery, gestational hypertension, preeclampsia, gestational diabetes, and perinatal morbidity and mortality [9–11]. Multiple pregnancy significantly increases all of these risks; therefore, single embryo transfer is the method of choice for ART procedures in women of ARA. If the woman in the case presentation above had significant health issues, including hypertension, diabetes, cardiovascular disease, a uterine anomaly, a vertically transmissible disease, phospholipid antibody syndrome, or other medical condition that would increase her risk for a poor outcome, proceeding with oocyte donation might result in significant harm to either the mother or the infant. In that clinical situation, it would be reasonable to either decline therapy for this couple or to consider a gestational carrier for the couple.

In an effort to reduce the perinatal risks for patients of ARA, all women in their 50s should be encouraged to undergo comprehensive medical testing that focuses on the assessment of cardiovascular and metabolic fitness. The age and health of the partner must also be considered. If risk factors are identified, properly counseling

---

[1] Editors' note – the author uses the terms female and woman as these terms are commonly used in the literature. However we recognize these issues affect persons whether they identify as female, male, or non-binary.

couples regarding these risks is imperative. In this regard, the assistance of a maternal fetal medicine (MFM) specialist may be warranted. Unfortunately, the data upon which to create precise risk-related counseling for all outcomes in this regard are limited.

The issues of frailty and the physical ability of the couple to care for a child until adulthood need to be considered. However, it is difficult to predict the health of an individual from age 52 until age 70, the age that the female partner in the case will be when her child turns 18. Nevertheless, this issue needs to be seriously discussed with the couple. In addition, the impact that advanced parental age will have on their child needs to be discussed. Unfortunately, there is a significant chance that a child born as a result of oocyte donation in our case scenario may experience the loss of one or both parents before reaching adulthood which could expose the child to harm [12].

Justice

The concept of justice in regard to medical treatments is defined as the need for fairness both in the distribution of scarce resources but also in the ability to meaningfully proceed with reproductive autonomous choice. Very few members of our population can access a cycle in later years as in the case of our 52-year-old patient. This inequity in access is highly problematic from an ethics standpoint. Moreover, the pregnancy and birth in this case will likely require a higher level of care, including likely neonatal care, beyond that which is typically needed for births during reproductive years. Given these concerns, many countries outside the United States have strict limits on access to state funded ART. That said, other countries, notably India, have few regulations. Denying one individual access to ART at any given age assuming they are healthy may violate the principle of autonomy, yet it is a common result of rationing in most other areas of medicine. Under our utilitarian principles, we commonly ration scarce resources to ensure access for the most people. All that said, assuming a healthy individual, it is likely ethical to proceed with a donated oocyte cycle even at ARA.

Conclusions

The patient in this case presentation is an older woman with higher risks in pregnancy, but she is three years younger than the age the ASRM guidelines say IVF should be "discouraged," has no comorbidities (e.g., hypertension or diabetes) and is overall in excellent health [13]. Weighing all factors discussed, it is ethically permissible in the case above to offer an oocyte donation cycle and potentially a gestational carrier if the patient and family wish to avoid the risks of gestation. Reproductive health care professionals will need to be aware of how inequitable access to this option is and should work to ensure a more just system of distribution of this scarce resource. Many of the factors considered above and weighing in favor of proceeding forward center around funding both for the cycle itself, for medical care and for raising children. Health care professionals also could ethically conclude that they would not offer oocyte donation cycles in this instance given the justice issues that are present. However, this might in turn require consideration of referral to another clinic if another clinic would be willing to proceed. Notably, there are few clinics in the United States that will offer IVF and transfer after a maternal age of 55. But there are clinics worldwide that will offer this care.

One must be aware that although the use of donor oocytes in patients with ARA results in acceptable pregnancy and delivery rates, this is not the case in patients who are of ARA, have diminished ovarian reserve, and want to use their own oocytes for assisted reproduction. In that clinical situation, the chance for a live birth after one IVF cycle is quite low. For example, based on the 2023 CDC assisted reproduction success rates estimator, a 45-year-old with diminished ovarian reserve, who has had one prior birth in her lifetime, has only a 3% chance for a live birth after one IVF cycle using her own oocytes [14]. Therefore, these patients need to be counseled regarding the very low chances for a live birth when using their own oocytes, and not given false hope for success.

The issues raised in the case presented above touch on concerns of ageism. With this in mind, health care professionals must consider how their personal and professional values shape the plans they propose. If a health care professional thinks that their values may be a barrier to the patient's access to care, this should prompt referral to a colleague. That said, concern for real risks in pregnancy at advanced age should not be equated with ageism per se. Autonomy is not a concept that would allow all persons to take on any and all risks. Given the common goal of a healthy infant, consideration of risks of advanced maternal age to the pregnant person and the eventual child are reasonable considerations and potential ethical barriers to proceeding.

Works Cited

1. Kawwass JF, Monsour M, Crawford S, Kissin DM, Session DR, Kulkarni AD, et al. Trends and outcomes for donor oocyte cycles in the United States, 2000-2010. JAMA 2013; 310:2426–34.
2. Kawwass JF, Crawford S, Hipp HS, Boulet SL, Kissin DM, Jamieson DJ, et al. Embryo donation: national trends and outcomes, 2000 through 2013. Am J Obst Gynecol 2016; 215:747.e1–5.
3. Sauer MV, Paulson RJ, Lobo RA. Pregnancy after 50: application of oocyte donation to women after natural menopause. Lancet 1993; 341:321–3. 2. 3.
4. Paulson RJ, Thornton MH, Francis MM, Salvador HS. Successful pregnancy in a 63-year-old woman. Fertil Steril 1997; 67:949–51.
5. Oocyte or embryo donation to women of advanced reproductive age: an Ethics Committee opinion. Fertil Steril 2016; 106:e3–7
6. Yeh JS, Steward RG, Dude AM, Shah AA, Goldfarb JM, Muasher SJ. Pregnancy rates in donor oocyte cycles compared to similar autologous in vitro fertilization cycles: an analysis of 26,457 fresh cycles from the Society for Assisted Reproductive Technology. Fertil Steril 2014; 102:399–404.

7. https://www.asrm.org/globalassets/asrm/asrm-content/news-and-publications/ethics-commit-tee-opinions/child-rearing_ability_and_the_provision_of_fertiilty_services.pdf
8. American College of Obstetrians and Gynecologists. ACOG Committee Opinion No. 762: Prepregnancy Counseling. Obstet Gynecol 2019; 133:e78–e89.
9. Kort DH, Gosselin J, Choi JM, Thornton MH, Cleary-Goldman J, Sauer MV. Pregnancy after age 50: defining risks for mother and child. Am J Perinatol 2012; 29:245–50.
10. Dulitski M, Soriano D, Schiff E, Chetrit A, Mashiach S, Seidman DS. Effect of very advanced maternal age on pregnancy outcome and rate of cesarean delivery. Obstet Gynecol 1998; 92:935–9.
11. Antinori S, Gholami GH, Versaci C, Cerusico F, Dani L, Antinori M, et al. Obstetric and pre-natal outcome in menopausal women: a 12-year clinical study. Reprod Biomed Online 2003; 6:257–61.
12. Melhem NM, Walker M, Moritz G, Brent DA. Antecedents and sequelae of sudden parental death in offspring and surviving caregivers. Arch Pediatr Adolesc Med. 2008; 162(5):403–410.
13. Fisseha S and Clark NA. Assisted Reproduction for Postmenopausal Women. Case and Commentary. AMA Journal of Ethics, Jan 2014.
14. CDC IVF success rate estimator, 2023.

Posthumous Gamete Collection and Use

Katherine Cameron and Samantha Butts

Abstract This chapter summarizes and weighs ethical issues surrounding posthumous gamete or embryo use while proposing guidelines and suggestions for how clinicians involved in assisted reproduction can best respect the rights of the deceased and surviving loved ones when the issue of posthumous reproduction is raised. The chapter covers scenarios including when the deceased's wishes are known regarding previously cryopreserved gametes or embryos, when wishes are unknown regarding previously cryopreserved embryos, when wishes are unknown regarding previously cryopreserved gametes, and when no gametes or embryos have been previously cryopreserved. There are many ethical challenges related to the use of posthumous gametes and embryos for procreation, both when they are already cryopreserved and when retrieval is necessary. For reproductive tissue already frozen, much consternation on the part of the physician and the surviving partner can be alleviated by having clearly delineated consent forms that include use of gametes after the death of one or both partners. While the presence of cryostored gametes or embryos shows that a parental project existed, it does not definitively demonstrate that the deceased accepted the continuation of the project after their death, and while perhaps ethically permissible providers should proceed with great caution.

Keywords Posthumous reproduction · Posthumous gametes · Posthumous embryos · Cryopreservation · Informed consent

K. Cameron (✉)
Division of Reproductive Endocrinology and Infertility, Johns Hopkins University School of Medicine, Baltimore, MD, USA

S. Butts
Division of Reproductive Endocrinology and Infertility, Penn State Health and Penn State College of Medicine, Hershey, PA, USA

© The Author(s), under exclusive license to Springer Nature Switzerland AG 2023
L. P. King, I. C. Band (eds.), *Case Studies in the Ethics of Assisted Reproduction*, https://doi.org/10.1007/978-3-031-41215-8_9

Case

A 40-year-old G0P0 woman presents at the fertility clinic for counseling. Her 50-year-old husband died 9 months prior unexpectedly from a heart attack. They had been undergoing IVF prior to his death and had cryopreserved embryos for use in future cycles. Though her husband had not authorized the use of the embryos after his death, the patient believes that he would have wanted her to conceive with the embryos. The reproductive endocrinologist is concerned that the patient's decision is clouded by grief and that she has no written consent from the husband for use of the embryo.

Scope of the Question

This chapter will summarize and weigh ethical issues surrounding posthumous gamete or embryo use while proposing guidelines and suggestions for how clinicians involved in assisted reproduction might respond to a scenario similar to the one described above. Posthumous reproduction can take place in two main scenarios, though many of the ethical questions are similar: (1) when cryopreservation of gametes or fertilization and cryopreservation of embryos takes place prior to the death of the partner, but the pregnancy occurs after the death of one of the partners, as described in the scenario above, versus (2) when procurement of gametes, fertilization, and pregnancy take place after the death of one of the partners. This chapter will address both scenarios, focusing on differences in considerations for the deceased. In addition, this chapter will highlight additional concerns for the oncofertility patient population, given that fertility preservation in this group is often undertaken in young individuals with a high risk of mortality from their disease.

Background

Posthumous conception of a child after the death of one or both gamete providers has been a possibility since the advent of gamete cryopreservation. The earliest cases involved posthumous sperm extraction, with the first case of posthumous sperm retrieval and storage reported in 1980 [1], and the first child being born using posthumously procured sperm from a man who died suddenly in 1997 [2]. In general, several options exist and are in current use allowing for cryopreservation of reproductive tissues. Sperm can be obtained by ejaculation, surgical excision from the epididymis, aspiration of the vas deferens and electroejaculation. These options are feasible both for men cryopreserving in the face of gonadotoxic treatment and as treatments for infertility. Sperm can also be retrieved from the body of a man after his death. For the female, follicular aspiration with cryopreservation of mature oocytes allows individuals to cryopreserve gametes. Biopsy and cryopreservation of ovarian tissue is available in some clinics, primarily for individuals facing gonado-toxic threats, as the ideal clinical application of this technology is still under investigation. Also, many infertile couples cryopreserve embryos for use in future in vitro fertilization (IVF) treatment cycles. The ability to obtain and cryopreserve gametes, reproductive tissue, and embryos has opened up possibilities and allowed for new permutations of posthumous reproduction.

In most cases, men or women who cryopreserve their gametes or embryos expect to be alive when the materials are used. However, an individual may authorize the use of stored materials after death. In the least controversial scenario, when children are conceived using cryopreserved gametes that were obtained prior to the death of the gamete provider, and explicit informed consent has been given to allow for use of the gamete for creation of a child after the death of the gamete provider, multiple professional organizations – including the American Society for Reproductive Medicine (ASRM) and the European Society of Human Reproduction and Embryology (ESHRE) – are supportive of posthumous reproduction [3, 4]. Some scholars object to posthumous reproduction even in this scenario, primarily out of concerns for the future offspring [5–9].

More problematic, however, is when explicit written informed consent is not available for posthumous reproduction. In this situation there are additional ethical considerations that must be considered to protect the rights and interests of the parties involved, including those of the deceased.

Ethical Considerations

Rights and Concerns of the Deceased

In considering the possible rights and concerns of the deceased involved in a parental project, a primary consideration is how potential rights change when an individual is no longer living. While traditionally the ethical principle of autonomy, or respect for one's wishes, has been the guiding principle in medical ethics, some ethicists have argued that the deceased no longer have any rights that need to be considered [10], given that the deceased cannot participate in the experience of child-rearing. However, there is precedent for still assigning moral weight to the wishes of the deceased – as examples, we uphold and enact wills and organ donation cards. Therefore, our society has chosen to respect the explicit wishes of the deceased and has attributed moral value to those wishes, and it can be argued that the same should be true for posthumous reproduction. By contrast, other societies may reach different conclusions. Notably in some parts of Asia and in Israel, given the weight assigned to continuing familial lines, posthumous reproduction without formal consent of the deceased is seen more favorably.[1]

When the Deceased's Wishes Are Known Regarding Previously Cryopreserved Gametes or Embryos

As discussed, when an individual has left explicit instructions that they wish to enter into a parental project with a partner, even after their death, and those wishes are in alignment with the surviving spouse/partner, there are few ethical concerns with the exception of the well-being of the potential offspring. There is evidence from small survey studies that a significant proportion of the general population find posthumous use of gametes morally acceptable in this situation [5, 11], as do the ASRM and ESHRE ethical societies [3, 4]. It should of course be noted that a desire from an individual for posthumous use of gametes or embryos should only be carried out in the setting of the living partner being willing to carry out the parental project, and the wishes of the deceased are not compulsory for the living.

When Wishes Are Unknown Regarding Previously Cryopreserved Embryos

When there is no pre-existing explicit consent regarding posthumous use of previously cryopreserved embryos, it is less clear how to proceed. The ASRM Ethics Committee states that "when embryos were created for the purpose of allowing a couple to reproduce together, in the absence of a written directive prohibiting the use of cryopreserved embryos by the surviving partner, it seems reasonable to allow surviving partners to reproduce from embryos [they] helped to create for that purpose unless there is other evidence that indicates that this would have been opposed by the deceased." This is more controversial, as in the absence of explicit consent it is impossible to truly know the wishes of the deceased. Reflecting this, the ESHRE Task Force on Ethics and Law states "in the absence of written consent, as in most cases of accidental persistent vegetative state or death, no action to obtain reproductive material can be performed, and no use can be made of the…embryos." In the absence of evidence that the deceased would have been opposed, it may be argued that it is reasonable to proceed given that the deceased took the positive action to cryopreserve embryos with his/her partner for future use. Furthermore, even without being able to confirm with the deceased their specific wishes, as a society we recognize that there is a primitive desire for reproduction as a means to create a

---

[1] Editors' note: See "Further Reading" section at end of chapter for more cross-cultural analysis of posthumous reproduction.

human heir. This is common to all cultures, religions, and social classes, and may allow us to reasonably conclude that creation of an heir from pre-existing embryos, even posthumously, may reflect a person's value structure [12]. Yet, respect for autonomy would lead us to favor a conservative approach and demand reliable affirmation of this desire. Thus, it is recommended that consent forms for IVF include a discussion of this eventuality so as to ensure a clear expression of the desires of both parties should one pre-decease the other.

When Wishes Are Unknown Regarding Previously Cryopreserved Gametes

Somewhat more difficult is how to handle gametes, not embryos, that were cryopreserved prior to death without explicit instructions for use. Again, the ASRM provides some guidance, stating that "in some cases the act of cryopreserving the gametes suggests a joint reproductive desire, which can be brought to fulfillment by the surviving partner. In other cases, gametes may have been cryopreserved outside of the partners' relationship with one another. After death, where there is evidence that the deceased would still have wanted reproduction to occur, or at least would not have objected, it seems reasonable to allow the survivor to proceed." Again, in this case, the positive action of cryopreserving gametes may demonstrate a desire for an heir that may be honored posthumously in the absence of evidence that this is not what the deceased would have wanted. Yet, the ideal protection of autonomy would involve a clear expression of these desires which can be accomplished during the consent process. Circling back to our prior example, we have an opt in system of organ donation. We do not presume in our country that persons would wish to donate their organs to the benefit of others.

In certain cases, a deceased individual may have left instructions that they do not wish for their gametes or embryos to be used after their passing. It may be argued that the deceased does not have an experiential claim to the gametes or embryos. This is particularly difficult in circumstances where the surviving partner wishes to use the gametes/embryos and they may be the survivor's only chance to have a biologically related child.[2] However, as above there is moral precedent for honoring the deceased wishes, and in such cases, the wishes of the deceased are clear, and thus the deceased has an interest in not reproducing that outweighs the survivor's interest in using the embryos or gametes to have a biologically related child.

Finally, there may arise a situation in which an individual with an interest in posthumous reproduction and cryopreserved gametes dies without an intended partner. In this case, the interests of the deceased are not buoyed by the shared aspiration

---

[2] Editors' note: For an example see https://www.cbsnews.com/news/court-uk-woman-cant-use--frozen-embryo/ but also see https://www.theguardian.com/law/2022/jun/22/widower-ted-jennings-wins-right-to-have-baby-with-embryo-created-with-his-late-wife

of a surviving partner, and ASRM states that the case for posthumous use of gametes is far less compelling. However others have argued that it may be acceptable for other family members (for instance, a sibling with infertility) to utilize the gametes in certain circumstances [13]. As noted previously, respect for the autonomy of the deceased likely argues in favor of a consent process that addresses these possibilities so that intent of the deceased is clearly articulated and followed.

When No Gametes or Embryos Have Been Previously Cryopreserved

In cases when the deceased has left explicit wishes in favor of posthumous reproduction, acquiring postmortem sperm is not controversial. However, the vast majority of deaths in reproductive aged men are sudden, unexpected, and occur outside of fertility clinics. The presence of written documentation of the deceased's wishes or of previously cryopreserved gametes is unlikely. In these cases, fertility clinics should proceed with caution and attempt to determine the desires of the decedent. This may require participation from a multidisciplinary team and discussions with other family members besides the partner/spouse. The ASRM states that "providers should not provide posthumous assisted reproduction if there is evidence that the deceased would not have wanted it. Moreover, the Committee discourages posthumous assisted reproduction unless there is clear evidence that it would have comported with the decedent's wishes" [4].

In the absence of written consent for posthumous reproduction, it may be reasonable for a fertility clinic to decline to participate in a partner/spouse's request for posthumous harvesting of gametes. However, some have argued for a position of 'presumed consent' [14, 15], given that in the vast majority of cases prior written consent will be unavailable. This argument is empirically based on several studies demonstrating that most men asked to consider posthumous conception would support their partner's harvesting and use of sperm [11, 16, 17]. The ASRM ethics committee points out that the decision to retrieve gametes does not compel a fertility clinic to later use the gametes. Though the decision to harvest gametes must be made quickly, the decision to utilize them in a reproductive project can be made later after adequate counseling and ascertainment of the deceased's wishes if possible.[3]

These situations highlight the critical importance of capturing a patient's explicit posthumous wishes in consent form documentation by assisted reproduction clinics when gametes or embryos are cryopreserved. The ethical

---

[3] Editors' note: For an example with references to differing state opinions see https://www.stat-news.com/2019/05/20/judge-rules-parents-of-deceased-west-point-cadet-can-decide-what-happens-with-his-sperm/

principle of autonomy cannot be guaranteed to be protected when the individual's wishes are unknown.

Rights and Concerns of the Surviving Spouse/ Reproductive Partner

There is no moral obligation for a surviving spouse or partner to utilize cryopreserved gametes/embryos in the event of the death of a partner. However, in the example scenario at the beginning of this section, while the spouse does intend to use the embryos, the physician appropriately feels concern for the surviving spouse and her decision-making abilities. The question may arise whether the surviving spouse can make a decision regarding continuing a parental project in the face of extreme grief. The process of bereavement includes both feelings of guilt and idealization of the deceased that may lead a surviving spouse to feel compelled to attempt to complete a parental project. These survivors need time and counseling to reach a reasoned decision regarding whether to proceed. European studies have demonstrated that a large majority of the requests made immediately after the death of the partner to use sperm are not followed up after a few months, and ESHRE suggests an obligatory minimum waiting period of a year to prevent "hasty and ill-considered decisions." Psychological counseling for surviving partners is of utmost importance to ensure support through the grieving process and a carefully considered decision. A clinical decision-making tool has been proposed to guide providers handling requests for posthumous reproduction from surviving spouses that focuses on facilitating communication [18].

Rights and Concerns of the Future Child

Physicians may have concerns for the well-being of the future child. These may be based on several factors, including that the child will be raised by one parent.

Concerns about the effect of single parenthood on development of the offspring can be examined and rejected with evidence from the social sciences. Both the absence of a father figure to assist in the emotional development of the child, and the possible financial disadvantage of single parenthood have been raised and have been refuted. There is strong evidence that children from single parent families are not disadvantaged in their emotional development [19]. Studies about the impact on children of the early death of a parent indicate that parental death is traumatic but that the negative consequences can be minimized by appropriate social support and providing clear and honest information about the circumstances of the parent's death [20]. Furthermore, some have raised concerns about children conceived from posthumous reproduction being treated as 'commemorative children', or a symbolic replacement for the deceased mother or father, that would have a detrimental effect on the child's well-being [3]. However, even in the cases of couples that have lost a child and have gone on to have another child, there is good evidence that the later-born children are treated properly and loved as the unique beings they are [21]. It is therefore unlikely that a child born after the death of the parent would be treated in a 'commemorative' way that was detrimental.

While it is reasonable for a physician to consider the welfare of the child, the bar to refuse care on these grounds is high. Clinics may only refuse to provide assisted reproduction out of concern for the well-being of the future child only if there are well grounded reasons for thinking that patients will be unable to provide minimally adequate or safe care for offspring [22].

Special Considerations for Oncofertility Population

In the field of oncofertility the need for prior discussion of a patient's wishes and written consent is extremely important, as these patients face an illness with risk of imminent mortality. In rare cases, there may be additional reproductive stakeholders beyond the original parental partner, including siblings or parents, who have an interest in future use of the gametes, especially in cases of a tragic death from malignancy in a relatively young individual. It is not unreasonable to envision for example a scenario in which a remaining spouse declines use of cryopreserved gametes, but a sibling facing health crises is interested in use of the gametes. In fact, in an effort to completely ascertain a patient's wishes, some clinics have recommended a 'roll-down' option that allows patients to delineate additional recipients, if the first listed on the consent form elects not to use the gametes. In the end, clear communication about a person's wishes ahead of their demise is the key to respecting their autonomy.

Conclusion

There are many ethical challenges related to the use of posthumous gametes and embryos for procreation, both when they are already cryopreserved and when retrieval is necessary. For reproductive tissue already frozen, much consternation on the part of the physician and the surviving partner can be alleviated by having clearly delineated consent forms that include use of gametes after the death of one or both partners. While the presence of cryostored gametes or embryos shows that a parental project existed, it does not definitively demonstrate that the deceased accepted the continuation of the project after their death, and while perhaps ethically permissible, providers should proceed with great caution.

References

1. Rothman CM. A method for obtaining viable sperm in the postmortem state. Fertil Steril 1980;34:512–2.
2. Allen JE. Woman pregnant by sperm from corpse. Associated Press 1998.
3. ESHRE Task Force on Ethics and Law, Pennings G, de Wert G, Shenfield F, Cohen J, Devroey P, et al. ESHRE Task Force on Ethics and Law 11: Posthumous assisted reproduction. Hum Reprod 2006;21:3050–3.
4. Ethics Committee of the American Society for Reproductive Medicine. Posthumous collection and use of reproductive tissue: a committee opinion. Fertil Steril 2018 Jul 1;110(1):45–49.
5. Bahadur G. Death and conception. Hum Reprod 2002;17:2769–75.
6. Landau R. Posthumous sperm retrieval for the purpose of later insemination or IVF in Israel: an ethical and psychosocial critique. Hum Reprod 2004;19:1952–6.
7. Orr RD, Siegler M. Is posthumous semen retrieval ethically permissible? J Med Ethics 2002;28:299–302.
8. Pobjoy J. Medically mediated reproduction: posthumous conception and the best interests of the child. J Law Med 2007;15:450–68.
9. White GB. Commentary: legal and ethical aspects of sperm retrieval. J Law Med Ethics 1999;27:359,61, 295.
10. Robertson JA. Posthumous reproduction. Indiana Law J 1994;69:1027–65.
11. Hans JD. Posthumous gamete retrieval and reproduction: would the deceased spouse consent? Soc Sci Med 2014;119:10–7.
12. Cote S, Affdal AO, Kadoch IJ, Hamet P, Ravitsky V. Posthumous reproduction with surplus in vitro fertilization embryos: a study exploring users' choices. Fertil Steril 2014;102:1410–5.
13. Dillon KE, Fiester AM. Sperm and oocyte cryopreservation: comprehensive consent and the protection of patient autonomy. Hum Reprod 2012;27:2894–8.
14. Tremellen K, Savulescu J. A discussion supporting presumed consent for posthumous sperm procurement and conception. Reprod Biomed Online 2015;30:6–13.
15. Tremellen K, Savulescu J. Posthumous conception by presumed consent. A pragmatic position for a rare but ethically challenging dilemma. Reprod Biomed Soc Online 2016;3:26–9.
16. Nakhuda GS, Wang JG, Sauer MV. Posthumous assisted reproduction: a survey of attitudes of couples seeking fertility treatment and the degree of agreement between intimate partners. Fertil Steril 2011;96:1463,1466.e1.
17. Pastuszak AW, Lai WS, Hsieh TC, Lipshultz LI. Posthumous sperm utilization in men presenting for sperm banking: an analysis of patient choice. Andrology 2013;1:251–5.
18. Panagiotopoulou N, Karavolos S. "Let Me Keep My Dead Husband's Sperm": Ethical Issues in Posthumous Reproduction. J Clin Ethics 2015;26:143–51.
19. Golombok S, Badger S. Children raised in mother-headed families from infancy: a follow-up of children of lesbian and single heterosexual mothers, at early adulthood. Hum Reprod 2010;25:150–7.
20. Ellis J, Dowrick C, Lloyd-Williams M. The long-term impact of early parental death: lessons from a narrative study. J R Soc Med 2013;106:57–67.
21. Grout LA, Romanoff BD. The myth of the replacement child: parents' stories and practices after perinatal death. Death Stud 2000;24:93–113.
22. Ethics Committee of American Society for Reproductive Medicine. Child-rearing ability and the provision of fertility services: a committee opinion. Fertil Steril 2013;100:50–3.

Further Reading (Cross-Cultural Perspectives About Posthumous Reproduction)

Diana, L. Y. H. (2013). Posthumous assisted reproduction in the East Asian context: towards a comprehensive framework of regulation. Asian Bioethics Review, 5(2), 93–109.

Doan HT, Doan DTP, Duong NKT. Post-mortem Reproduction from a Vietnamese Perspective-an Analysis and Commentary. Asian Bioeth Rev. 2020;12(3):257–288. Published 2020 Aug 6. doi:https://doi.org/10.1007/s41649-020-00137-z

Hashiloni-Dolev Y. Posthumous Reproduction (PHR) in Israel: Policy Rationales Versus Lay People's Concerns, a Preliminary Study. Cult Med Psychiatry. 2015;39(4):634–650. doi:https://doi.org/10.1007/s11013-015-9447-6

Hashiloni-Dolev Y, Schicktanz S. A cross-cultural analysis of posthumous reproduction: The significance of the gender and margins-of-life perspectives. Reprod Biomed Soc Online. 2017;4:21–32. Published 2017 Apr 29. doi:https://doi.org/10.1016/j.rbms.2017.03.003

Anonymity and Other Concerns in Gamete Donation Assisted Reproduction

Karissa Hammer and Shruthi Mahalingaiah

Abstract A variety of ethical concerns arise related to gamete donation, including the issues of anonymity and health risks to the donor. Various stakeholder interests must be considered in any ethical analysis including those of the reproductive medicine professional, clinic/program, gamete recipient(s), gamete donor and resulting progeny. Recently, high profile cases in the media have made clear that complete anonymity is impossible to promise given technological advances (e.g., commercially available genetic testing), changing social norms (e.g., linkage sites and social media) and an evolving legal landscape. Informed consent must include a discussion of potential health risks associated with gamete donation (e.g., ovarian hyperstimulation) and of the fact that information-sharing policies are not guaranteed (i.e., donors may be contacted by offspring in the future). Donors and recipient(s) should also provide medical updates related to serious medical conditions that may impact the health of future children.

Keywords Anonymity · Gamete donation · Informed consent · Genetic testing · Linkage sites

K. Hammer
Institute for Human Reproduction, Chicago, IL, USA

S. Mahalingaiah (✉)
Department of Environmental Health, Harvard T.H. Chan School of Public Health, Boston, MA, USA

Department of OB/GYN, Division of Reproductive Endocrinology and Infertility, Massachusetts General Hospital, Boston, MA, USA

Case 1

A couple in their late thirties wants to have children but cannot conceive, and the 38-year-old male partner discovers through testing that he cannot produce gametes. Tests show that the female partner has no obvious concerns for infertility. The couple decides that they would like to use male donor gametes. During their consult, the couple expresses a desire to have the healthiest child possible and to be prepared to address any health risks their future child might be exposed to down the line. Therefore, the couple requests information about the donor's personal and family medical history, genetic and ancestral origins, ongoing information around the donor's health that may be relevant after the birth of their future child, biographical information about the donor including information about educational and professional accomplishments. Finally, the couple expresses desire to give their future child the option to contact the donor down the line, if they wish to. The selected donor had independently chosen to undergo genetic screening and donate his gametes anonymously to a sperm bank.

Case 2

Similar in all respects to Case 1 however, the gametes required are oocytes. While donation of sperm carries few health related risks, donation of oocytes can involve risks including ovarian hyperstimulation.

Scope of the Question

This chapter will summarize and weigh ethical concerns surrounding anonymity in gamete donation balanced against potential health risks. These concepts involve the interests, rights and duties of involved parties: physician or reproductive medicine professional, clinic/program (collecting/storing/distributing donations), gamete recipient(s), gamete donor (including potential health related concerns of donation) and resulting progeny. The legal landscape for gamete donor anonymity is ever-evolving due to rapidly changing social standards and technology advances. Complete anonymity is impossible to promise. These concepts will be reviewed within the reproductive timeline for gamete donation and within a framework of ethical principles including autonomy, beneficence, non-maleficence and justice.

Background

The ethical concerns of this chapter revolve around anonymity, which is directly tied with information sharing. There are varying levels of information sharing in gamete donation. Traditionally, involved parties could choose to have [1] non-identifying information sharing, which ends at de-identified medical and social history, [2] non-identifying contact information for medical updates, by which the donor and recipient(s) can communicate high impact medical updates to the other party in an effort to protect the long-term health of involved parties, [3] identifying information, which explicitly allows potential offspring the option of contacting the donor [1]. However, with the advent of online genetic testing and linkage websites, complete anonymity can no longer be guaranteed.

Reproductive Time Arc

The act of gamete donation, although a single event, has an impact on many future occurrences and lives. In this section we review the reproductive time arc involved in gamete donation: donor selection, fertility outcomes, perinatal health/early childhood and long-term health outcomes. In addition to the reproductive timeline for the recipient and offspring, we review a possible reproductive timeline of the donor.

Donor Selection

The process for a recipient(s) of donor gametes begins with the donor selection. As described in the above cases, recipient(s) search for very specific details about gamete donors as they hope the described characteristics and health information about the donor will help predict and plan for their future offspring. Programs typically have levels of information that are offered for various fees, though the basic information is freely available. This essential level of information provides a thorough description of the donor that may include basic medical history; detailed physical descriptions of the donor (height, weight, eye color, hair color, texture and volume, body frame, complexion); religious affiliations; education level/achievement; reported athletic, mathematical and mechanical skills; hobbies; languages spoken and likes/dislikes. At higher levels of payment to the program, recipient(s) can view the donor's childhood photos, adult photos, have a conversation with the donor or hear voice recordings and even see results of a personality test [2, 3]. All of this anonymous information is potentially available for the recipient(s) to view prior to making a purchase of a donor's gametes. Additionally, the recipient(s) can see whether the donor has agreed to being identified by the recipient(s) or offspring in the future.

The donor may make requests regarding who may or may not receive their gametes, however, the program then also has the right to refuse their donation [1]. Most often, donors do not have the opportunity to select the recipient(s) features or traits; instead, the promise of anonymity blinds them to this process.

Fertility Outcome

Once the recipient(s) receive the anonymously donated gametes, they undergo respective fertility treatment. In the case at hand (case 1), the donor gamete would be a semen sample which would be used either for intrauterine insemination or *in vitro* fertilization (IVF). The outcome of this process may be considered successful and lead to a pregnancy or unsuccessful with either a miscarriage or no conception. Regardless, the anonymous donor is not typically notified of these outcomes.

If the recipient(s) becomes pregnant, the details of this pregnancy including any complications and the birth of a child (or children) is information most often kept to the family and their healthcare professionals and is not revealed to the donor. In the case at hand, the intended parents ask for ongoing medical information about the donor. The following question then arises: should the same be provided for the donor? Should they be informed of potential fertility concerns, pregnancy outcomes and live births related to their gamete donation? This information could have implications for the donor's personal health, future fertility and own offspring yet is typically not shared.

Perinatal Health/Early Childhood

The parents in this chapter's case describe the lengths they would go to for a healthy child, which include seeking out information about the donor in the future. Should the same expectation for ongoing health information exist in the reverse such that the recipient(s)'s fertility outcomes and offspring's health outcomes be shared with the donor? This information has potential to impact the fertility of the donor and the health of their future offspring. Prior to donating, the recipient(s) and donors undergo genetic testing. This can vary widely from ten to hundreds of genetically linked disease processes. If offspring were to develop a disease with genetic underpinnings, there is no legal requirement that this information be disclosed to the program, clinic or donor [4].

Long Term Health Outcomes

While the genetic screening of the donor and recipient(s) is extensive, it is by no means a fool-proof way of preventing future genetic disease processes. Our understanding of the human genome is evolving. At present, the American College of Obstetricians and Gynecologists (ACOG) recommends that anyone considering pregnancy or already pregnant be at minimum screened for "cystic fibrosis, spinal muscular atrophy, thalassemias and hemoglobinopathies" and any additional screening based on the individual's personal or family history [5]. Genetic tests for donors can range from ten diseases to hundreds if an expanded genetic carrier panel is performed. Appropriately, counseling on the option of genetic screening of donor and recipient(s) of donor gametes should be provided by the REI clinic and/or gamete donation center. It must also be discussed that these tests are not predictive of all future diseases as we are still learning about the human genome and the various expressions of diseases. Many disease processes that occur later in life such as heart disease and cancer are not predictive from these tests [6]. In the chapter's case, the intended parents wanted ongoing health information about their donor in order to optimize their offspring's health. Does this cross the line of anonymity if the donor's health information can be anonymously provided? Similarly, if the offspring develops an illness that could potentially also impact the donor's own offspring, should the communication be provided to the donor [4]? How fluid should these lines of communication be, and should the physician make those connections? Is it their ethical responsibility to do so?

Donor Reproductive Timeline

At the time of gamete donation, the donor is likely to be in the prime of their health during their reproductive years. These individuals sign contractual agreements dictating what may occur with their donated gametes. For example, the donor can determine whether or not their gametes can be used for research purposes or disposed of after a designated period of time. In cases where contractual agreements have not been upheld, legal cases have arisen. A donor who donated his sperm for research and/or no more than five offspring sued his clinic after discovering through online genetic testing that he had upwards of 15 offspring [7]. This example stresses the importance of informed consent and upholding the contracted agreement for use of donated specimens.

Most often, after donation, no further communication occurs between the anonymous donor and the program/clinic unless otherwise specified in the contract. There are some scenarios, however, that bring this anonymity and loss of rights of genetic material into question. For example, if a male donor develops testicular cancer and loses both gonads, should he be able to contact the program to access his previously cryopreserved gametes? Additionally, should there be a time limit for which gametes are cryopreserved, particularly after a donor is deceased?

Ethical Considerations

Autonomy

Maintaining the principle of autonomy in gamete donation is complex as it concerns each individual involved: donor, recipient(s) and potential progeny.

To donate gametes, donors must agree to a list of medical tests that involve testing for infectious diseases, genetic screening, medical history screening and social history screening. Prior to proceeding with this screening and donation, the individual is thoroughly counseled on the decisions they must make regarding their gametes; the decisions involve degree of anonymity with recipient(s) and offspring, use of donated gametes for biomedical research, disposal of unused gametes, and willingness for de-identified contact for updated medical information in the future. The individual donor is counseled on the potential future psychological and emotional impact of donation. As noted above, in exchange for a fee, donors give up a great deal of autonomous decision making regarding the disposition of their gametes and all decision making regarding genetically related children.

For recipient(s), autonomy is respected in their choice of gamete donor. When an individual chooses, or is recommended medically, to use donor gametes, they have the opportunity to search for a donor who reflects the physical characteristics, social history, genetic background and medical history. The recipient(s) also has the autonomy to determine whether to inform their child of their conception by gamete donation [8]. While the American Society of Reproductive Medicine (ASRM) has "encouraged recipient parent(s) to disclose the fact of gamete donation to children, and a number of clinics provide for some form of future contact between donor and child if the participants agree," the decision remains with the recipient(s) [1]. Thus, the autonomy of recipients is heavily prioritized.

Progeny from gamete donation also deserve respected autonomy. An individual may desire to know their ancestry, learn of other genetic relatives or even contact their donor. In the past, clinics favored upholding donors' requests for anonymity as this ensured a higher rate of donation than in other countries where anonymity was not guaranteed and donations were fewer. With increased availability of genetic testing via simple kits available from websites (i.e. 23andMe.com or ancestry.com), complete anonymity of donors is nearly impossible. Informed consent of the donor and recipient(s) must include the discussion of this potential.

Beneficence and Non-maleficence

Medical professionals providing reproductive healthcare aim to provide benefit to all parties involved and to society at large. In gamete donation, the goal is to minimize risk to the donor, offer an opportunity for a healthy offspring for the recipient(s) and provide potential for a healthy future for resulting offspring. The greater implication of "do good" for gamete donation is the impact on society. Providers must track and understand the larger impact gamete donation may have; for example, multiple gifts from the same donor may lead to inadvertent consanguinity or negative psychological impact for the donor if they are to learn of or are contacted by multiple progeny in the future. ASRM has advised limits for sperm donors to "no more than 25 pregnancies per sperm donor in a population of 800,000 to minimize the risk of consanguinity" and has limited the number of stimulated oocyte donations for a female donor to six [9]. Physicians and clinics are responsible not only for tracking outcomes but also for making appropriate practice changes to reflect the good of society as a whole. For example, ASRM has tracked the future ovarian reserve of oocyte donors and has not found a decrease due to previous donations [9]. However, if they were to find an impact on future fertility, the practice of oocyte donation should change.

Health care professionals have an obligation to respect the donor's expressed wishes for a degree of anonymity in the donation process. However, such anonymity cannot be guaranteed, and legislation around this topic is frequently changing, most recently making anonymity no longer available in some countries in response to the UN Convention on the Rights of the Child. [1] Thus, the primary duty of health care professionals to donors is to ensure they are well informed about the impermanence of anonymity.

Moreover, there are scenarios which require a breach in anonymity. For example, if a donor's gametes lead to future progeny that develop a medical condition that could negatively impact the donor's own offspring, the healthcare professional could ethically break anonymity to discuss these outcomes with the donor. A similar scenario may occur where a donor develops a serious medical condition that could potentially be genetically linked and impact the recipient(s) offspring; similarly, in this scenario, the beneficent act would be for the donor to break anonymity and report this to the clinic and/or recipient(s).

A further duty for healthcare professionals would be to ensure safe procedures for donors. For males, donation is a physically low risk process. Donation is more invasive for females, however risk of serious complication occurs in less than 0.5% of cases [9]. Routine safety processes must be maintained and the female donor must be appropriately screened for the procedure of ovarian stimulation and oocyte retrieval. The emotional and psychological risks may be minimized with appropriate counseling and informed decision making.

---

[1] Editors' note: Please see ESHRE guidance https://academic.oup.com/hropen/article/2022/1/hoac001/6528996

For recipients, healthcare professionals have a duty to help provide gametes that have a potential to create healthy offspring through diligent screening processes for donors by reviewing genetic, medical and social histories that may impact pregnancy, birth and the offspring throughout a lifetime. All known factors that may contribute to these aspects of health must be disclosed to the recipient(s).

Justice

From a societal viewpoint, distributive justice of donor gametes is not upheld. The use of donor gametes requires a cost that may be prohibitive for many individual(s) who require them for reproductive purposes. Beyond costs, the tracking of offspring from donation is limited by anonymity such that programs are not always aware of the fertility outcomes of the donation. Accurate information tracking regarding gamete donation and potential offspring is of utmost importance, but anonymity can create a barrier to this process. For true distributive justice, access to needed gametes must be equitable, and the system of tracking donations and their outcomes must be improved.

Conclusion

There are multiple participants in gamete donation: reproductive medicine professional, clinic/program, society, donor, recipient(s) and potential offspring. Balancing the ethical principles of autonomy, beneficence, non-maleficence and justice for all involved is complex. Social norms, medical knowledge, legal frameworks and technology will continue to change over time and as each does, we should be ready and willing to adapt our scope for discussing these ethical scenarios.

ASRM recommends that "programs should caution participants that policies related to information sharing are not guaranteed since laws or individual circumstances change and that there is a possibility that they may be contacted by offspring in the future. Similarly, maintaining anonymity of parties cannot be guaranteed since commercially available genetic testing ad agencies that allow dissemination of identifying information through social media increases the risk of inadvertent disclosure of participants." [1] They also strongly encourage donors and recipient(s) to provide "medical updates" related to serious medical conditions that may impact the health of the donor's future children or recipient's children.

Works Cited

1. Ethics Committee of the American Society for Reproductive Medicine. Electronic address aao, Ethics Committee of the American Society for Reproductive M. Interests, obligations, and rights in gamete and embryo donation: an Ethics Committee opinion. Fertil Steril 2019;111:664–70.
2. Donor Search. Generate Life Sciences. (Accessed 5/22/20, at https://www.cryobank.com/search/.)
3. Donor Search. 2020. (Accessed 05/22/2020, at https://fairfaxcryobank.com/search/.)
4. Cha AE. The children of Donor H898. The Washington Post 2019 September 14, 2019.
5. Committee on G. Committee Opinion No. 690: Carrier Screening in the Age of Genomic Medicine. Obstet Gynecol 2017;129:e35–e40.
6. Screen MFC. Myriad Foressight Carrier Screen. Universal Panel Disease List. 2019.
7. Toropin TWaK. A doctor donated sperm 30 years ago. Now he has at least 17 kids, lawsuit alleges. CNN 2019.
8. Ethics Committee of the American Society for Reproductive Medicine. Electronic address Aao, Ethics Committee of the American Society for Reproductive M. Informing offspring of their conception by gamete or embryo donation: an Ethics Committee opinion. Fertil Steril 2018;109:601–5.
9. Practice Committee of the American Society for Reproductive M, Practice Committee of the Society for Assisted Reproductive T. Repetitive oocyte donation: a committee opinion. Fertil Steril 2014;102:964 6.

Third Party Reproduction

Isabelle C. Band and Louise P. King

Abstract This chapter explores ethical issues pertinent to third party reproduction, including autonomy, beneficence and non-maleficence. Use of a gestational carrier is one path forward when individuals who wish to become parents to genetically related children are unable to gestate for a variety of medical or social reasons. The practice is controversial and illegal in some countries. While in a neutral setting, individuals can autonomously consent to gestate for another intended parent, critics of the practice suggest that in certain social, economic, and geographic scenarios, offering compensation to gestational carriers undermines truly voluntary informed consent. The most compelling argument in support of third-party reproduction relates to beneficence: the practice provides a family-building option for single men, same-sex male couples, and persons with uteri for whom gestating a child is unsafe or medically impossible. However, pregnancy poses physical and psychological risks to gestational carriers and potentially to future children in international settings if the identity of their legal parents is contested. It is critical that gestational carriers provide meaningful informed consent and receive appropriate medical care and that intended parents and gestational carriers secure or are afforded independent legal counsel. According to the ASRM Ethics Committee, compensation for gestational carriers is ethically permissible, although a different conclusion has been reached internationally.

Keywords Third party reproduction · Surrogacy · Gestational carrier · Informed consent · Beneficence

I. C. Band (✉)
Icahn School of Medicine at Mount Sinai, New York, NY, USA

L. P. King
Center for Bioethics, Harvard Medical School, Boston, MA, USA

© The Author(s), under exclusive license to Springer Nature Switzerland AG 2023
L. P. King, I. C. Band (eds.), *Case Studies in the Ethics of Assisted Reproduction*, https://doi.org/10.1007/978-3-031-41215-8_11

Case

A 40-year-old G0P0 presents for fertility counseling. She and her male partner have been trying to become pregnant for the past year. She discovers after testing that she has extensive fibroids, and despite surgical intervention it is determined that her uterus is unlikely to carry pregnancy to term. The couple expresses their desire to have a biological child and requests that a gestational carrier be impregnated via IVF with an embryo created from their gametes.

Scope of the Question

This chapter will consider the ethical issues raised by third party reproduction. Use of a gestational carrier is an increasingly common practice that allows individuals to become parents despite circumstances in which carrying a pregnancy is medically impossible or contraindicated. Use of a gestational carrier occurs when a woman agrees to gestate a child for a couple or individual seeking these reproductive services to become the parent(s) of a child [1]. The woman who gestates the child is referred to as a gestational carrier while the individual(s) who seek the gestational carrier's services are referred to as the intended parent(s). Gestational carriers provide only gestation but not gametes for pregnancy [1].

The "gamete providers" may or may not be the intended parents (i.e. the intended parents may use their own gametes or donated ones), however the case analyzed in this chapter illustrates a scenario in which the intended parents use their own gametes [1]. Of note, this chapter will not discuss "traditional surrogacy," in which the surrogate provides the oocyte(s) and gestates the pregnancy. Traditional surrogacy poses significant ethical and legal complications and thus should be avoided (see "Further Reading" at end of chapter).

A range of opinions exist around the practice of payment for surrogacy. Arguments in support of payment for gestational carriers emphasize that each party should be free to exercise reproductive autonomy. However, arguments in opposition to payment for gestational surrogacy focus on potential for harm to the gestational carrier and resulting offspring. Others have opposed it because they regard contractual surrogacy as commodification of the body [1]. Still others have pointed to instances in which abuses have been well documented leading for example to banning the practice in India. This chapter will consider ethics as they pertain to the economic considerations associated with the gestational carrier arrangement.

Background

In vitro fertilization (IVF) has made it possible for physicians to transfer the embryo of intended parents into the uterus of a gestational carrier. This practice was first introduced in the 1980s, when it was used primarily by heterosexual couples who had fertility or medical problems that made the female partner unable to carry a child to term. More recently, the practice has been used increasingly often by individuals or same-sex couples to have biological children.

Between 2006 and 2015, the number of ART cycles that involved a gestational carrier more than doubled, from 2251 in 2006 to 4725 in 2015. The percentage of cycles using a gestational carrier increased from 2% in 2006 to more than 3% in 2015. The CDC's 2015 National Summary of ARTs found that 87% of clinics allowed cycles using gestational carriers [2]. Multiple longitudinal studies have demonstrated that gestational-carrier cycles resulted in higher rates of implantation, pregnancy, and live birth compared with non-gestational-carrier cycles [2–4].

Despite the increase in use of gestational surrogacy, it is important to note that U.S. surrogacy laws vary by state. For example, a Louisiana bill restricts gestational surrogacy to heterosexual married couples using their own gametes. There is a strict no compensation requirement, meaning that commercial surrogacy is prohibited in Louisiana. If one enters into a surrogacy agreement not sanctioned by this 2016 law, anyone involved is subject to civil and criminal penalties [5]. On the other hand, California permits commercial surrogacy, enforces gestational surrogacy contracts, and makes it possible for all intended parents, regardless of marital status or sexual orientation, to establish their legal parentage prior to birth and without adoption proceedings [6]. This chapter will primarily focus on the ethical rather than legal questions raised by gestational surrogacy and compensation for the practice.

Ethical Considerations

In order to address the pertinent ethical questions raised by the case, IVF clinics will likely consider key ethical principles including autonomy, beneficence and nonmaleficence. This chapter will elaborate on how each of these ethical principles apply to the case at hand.

Autonomy

A common argument for gestational surrogacy posits that consenting adults should have the freedom to engage in reproductive decision making and that this includes the right to consent to gestate for another intended parent and to receive compensation [1]. An individual's right to ask another to help them to reproduce is in turn constrained by the obligation to avoid harming the other involved parties including the potential child or the gestational carrier.

Individuals who are morally opposed to compensating gestational surrogates have also invoked autonomy in their arguments. There is often a significant socioeconomic gap between the gestational carrier and the intended parents. While the disparity does not always translate into "undue inducement" some have suggested that in certain social, economic and geographic scenarios, a given amount of compensation may be coercive [7]. Although a woman may consent to a gestational surrogacy agreement, her ability to provide consent free from coercion may be illusory given financial desperation. Financially destitute women may take on risks as a gestational surrogate because they see themselves as having no other realistic or viable options for supporting themselves or their families. It has been suggested that compensation may also dissuade a gestational surrogate from disclosing health conditions or family history [7].

Beneficence

The principal argument in favor of gestational surrogacy is that it gives individuals access to another way of having children. The discovery of not being able to gestate a child may be devastating and stressful for a woman or couple [7]. In addition, same-sex male couples and single men cannot have biologically related children without the service of a gestational carrier. While adoption is another possibility for the hopeful parents under discussion, adoption would give up the possibility of having a genetic link to one's child, which to some is valuable and important. Moreover, gestational surrogacy can provide a family-building option for single men, same-sex male couples, or women for whom gestating a child is unsafe or medically impossible. Benefits also may exist for the gestational surrogate who may enjoy the experience of pregnancy and who may derive satisfaction from being able to help others become biological parents [7].

Non-maleficence

Pregnancy can take a toll on an individual, both physically and psychosocially. For one, the gestational surrogate exposes herself to health risks by agreeing to be a surrogate. Unanticipated medical complications can arise including antenatal diagnosis of fetal disease for which treatment is invasive to the gestational carrier, as well as pregnancy-induced disease that may do harm to the fetus [7]. In addition, the gestational surrogate may face psychosocial stressors. During her pregnancy, the gestational carrier has frequent (often weekly) follow-up visits before she is discharged to regular obstetric care. Being pregnant may interfere with the surrogate's ability to continue in full-time employment, care for her own children (typically having had children is a requirement ahead of becoming a surrogate) and engage in other obligations or activities she might otherwise pursue [1].

In addition, others have made the argument that gestational surrogacy does harm by commodifying the gestational surrogate and childbirth itself [1]. Critics of surrogacy argue that payment for bodily services dehumanizes the surrogate and exploits her reproductive organs for the personal gain of others [8].

There is no conclusive data on whether being gestated by a gestational surrogate impacts the offspring psychologically or socially [9]. Although rare, there are a handful of cases in which gestational carriers have claimed parental rights over gestated offspring [10]. These scenarios can cause psychosocial harm and trauma to the offspring as well as the other involved parties. However, such scenarios can be avoided by providing the gestational carrier with counseling before, during and after the pregnancy and ensuring that there is an agreed upon contract in place between the intended parents and gestational carrier [1].

Conclusions

The ASRM and ACOG have published guidelines around the use of gestational carriers and have provided their recommendations regarding appropriate compensation. Both have emphasized that it is of the utmost importance that gestational carriers provide informed consent [1, 7]. Gestational carriers should be informed of the physical and psychosocial risks of the role. They also require appropriate medical care throughout the treatment and pregnancy. Although the interests of the intended parents are considerable, gestational carriers are the sole source of consent regarding their medical care. This is important to note, because complications of pregnancy can result in situations where fetal or neonatal well-being could be compromised to preserve maternal health [1]. OBGYNs who counsel individuals considering engaging in a gestational carrier agreement ought to encourage intended parents and gestational carriers to discuss as many scenarios as possible and plans for addressing complications that may arise during the pregnancy. If there is a lack of congruence or respect between the parties and their wishes, they ought not to engage in the agreement. If a disagreement arises during the pregnancy, the agreed-upon contract should prevail but ultimately the gestational carrier has authority around their body and cannot be compelled to undergo procedures [1].

Gestational carriers should have independent legal counsel that is distinct from the legal counsel of the intended parents. The intended parents must take all of the necessary legal steps to secure their status as the legal parents of the child and should also have counseling available to them throughout the process, especially before, to help them make an informed decision before deciding to enter a gestational carrier agreement, and in order to help them decide how, if at all, they want to disclose to the child at some point that they used a gestational carrier [1].

Finally, the ASRM suggests that compensation for gestational carriers is ethically permissible [1]. They argue that compensation for gestational surrogacy is consistent with compensation for other situations like participation in medical research that demand time, stress, physical effort and risk [1]. Gestational carriers ought to also receive healthcare coverage for pregnancy and receive compensation that accounts for nine months of possible illness and risks to employment. However, compensation should not create "undue inducement" or risks of exploitation [1]. To ensure that this is the case, carriers should be at least 21-years old, healthy, and have a stable social environment. The payment should adequately compensate women for the time, inconvenience, and risk associated with being a gestational carrier, and should not be contingent on the birth of a healthy child [1].

Works Cited

1. Daar J, Benward J, Collins L, et al. Consideration of the gestational carrier: an Ethics Committee opinion. *Fertil Steril*. 2018;110(6):1017–1021. https://doi.org/10.1016/j.fertnstert.2018.08.029
2. 2015 Assisted Reproductive Technology National Summary Report. Published online 2015:74.
3. Murugappan G, Farland LV, Missmer SA, Correia KF, Anchan RM, Ginsburg ES. Gestational carrier in assisted reproductive technology. *Fertil Steril*. 2018;109(3):420–428. https://doi.org/10.1016/j.fertnstert.2017.11.011
4. Perkins KM, Boulet SL, Jamieson DJ, Kissin DM. Trends and outcomes of gestational surrogacy in the United States. *Fertil Steril*. 2016;106(2):435–442.e2. https://doi.org/10.1016/j.fertnstert.2016.03.050
5. Gestational Surrogacy in Louisiana. Creative Family Connections. Accessed July 8, 2022. https://www.creativefamilyconnections.com/us-surrogacy-law-map/louisiana/
6. Tsai S, Shaia K, Woodward JT, Sun MY, Muasher SJ. Surrogacy Laws in the United States: What Obstetrician–Gynecologists Need to Know. *Obstet Gynecol*. 2020;135(3):717–722. https://doi.org/10.1097/AOG.0000000000003698
7. Family Building Through Gestational Surrogacy. Accessed July 8, 2022. https://www.acog.org/en/clinical/clinical-guidance/committee-opinion/articles/2016/03/family-building-through-gestational-surrogacy
8. Adamu C. Ethical Issues in Commercial Gestational Surrogacy. *AMAMIHE J Appl Philos*. 2020;18(4). https://doi.org/10.13140/RG.2.2.26043.64803
9. Jadva V, Imrie S. Children of surrogate mothers: psychological well-being, family relationships and experiences of surrogacy. *Hum Reprod*. 2014;29(1):90–96. https://doi.org/10.1093/humrep/det410
10. Daar J, Benward J, Collins L, et al. Misconduct in third-party assisted reproduction: an Ethics Committee opinion. *Fertil Steril*. 2018;110(6):1012–1016. https://doi.org/10.1016/j.fertnstert.2018.08.030

Further Reading

Deonandan R. Recent trends in reproductive tourism and international surrogacy: ethical considerations and challenges for policy. *Risk Management and Healthcare Policy*. 2015;8:111–119. https://doi.org/10.2147/RMHP.S63862
Lokshin V. Surrogacy -a worldwide demand. Implementation and ethical considerations. 2021;2(2):66–73.
Patel NH, Jadeja YD, Bhadarka HK, Patel MN, Patel NH, Sodagar NR. Insight into Different Aspects of Surrogacy Practices. *J Hum Reprod Sci*. 2018;11(3):212–218. https://doi.org/10.4103/jhrs.JHRS_138_17

Provision of Fertility Services Without Regard to Marital Status, Sexual Orientation or Gender Identity

Isabelle C. Band and Louise P. King

Abstract Assisted reproductive technologies (ART) make possible a range of alternative family structures (i.e., families with single, unmarried or LGBTQ+ parents). However, some practices still decline provision of ART to single and diverse sexuality and gender (DSG) individuals. Fertility clinics across the United States vary in terms of the options they provide to these patients (Wu et al., Fertil Steril 108(1):183–191, 2017). Those clinics who appropriately favor equal access to fertility services, regardless of marital status, sexual orientation, or gender identity, emphasize that single and DSG individuals often desire biologically related children and have the autonomy to seek out fertility care to support those interests. They emphasize justice (i.e., that different treatment is only justified when there is a morally relevant difference between cases) and the "right to reproduce" (De Wert et al., Hum Reprod Oxf Engl 29(9):1859–1865, 2014). Clinics who do not support equal access to fertility treatment question the welfare of children born into alternative family structures, despite clear evidence to undermine this concern, and inappropriately prioritize professional autonomy (APA, Published online 2004; van Rijn-van Gelderen, J Adolesc 40:65–73, 2015; Farr, Dev Psychol 53(2):252–264, 2017; Goldberg et al., J Fam Psychol 27(3):431–442, 2013). Marital status, sexual orientation and gender identity do not impact parenting ability and thus physicians have an ethical duty to treat unmarried and DSG individuals in the same manner as heterosexual married couples when determining which services to provide (ASRM Ethics Committee, Fertil Steril 116(2):326–330, 2021).

Keywords LGBTQ+ · Single parent · Gay · Lesbian · Transgender

I. C. Band (✉)
Icahn School of Medicine at Mount Sinai, New York, NY, USA

L. P. King
Center for Bioethics, Harvard Medical School, Boston, MA, USA

L. P. King, I. C. Band (eds.), *Case Studies in the Ethics of Assisted Reproduction*, https://doi.org/10.1007/978-3-031-41215-8_12

Case

A 40-year-old cisgender man and his 36-year-old cisgender male partner present for fertility counseling. They express a strong desire to have a child, who is biologically related to one of them. They are not currently married to one another, but plan to get married in the future. They state that they have both always wanted to raise children. They would like to pursue IVF with a donor egg and one of their sperm (they do not express a strong preference about which of them is the "biological father," they would just like to have the "healthiest possible" child), with the embryo transferred into a gestational carrier.

Scope of the Question

This chapter will provide a summary of the ethical considerations surrounding the provision of fertility services to single individuals, unmarried couples and diverse sexuality and gender (DSG) individuals and couples. Then, we will provide recommendations surrounding ethical provision of fertility services to such individuals.

Background

Assisted reproductive technologies technically make possible the creation of alternative family structures – family structures other than those with cisgender, heterosexual, married parents who are both biologically related to their children. However, in the 1980s and 1990s, during the early years of IVF, the technology was primarily used by white, heterosexual, married couples given its high cost and firmly-held ideals about the "natural" American family [1, 2]. LGBTQ+ individuals were "widely stigmatized in regard to family formation, deemed unworthy to reproduce, unfit for rearing children, and contrary to the very notions of parenthood and family." [3].

In the 2000s, a gradual shift occurred and lesbian women began having children through fertility industry-aided donor insemination [3]. Shortly thereafter, gay men began utilizing ARTs to have biological children, for whom the financial burden of family building is especially high given the need to compensate both an egg donor and gestational carrier [3, 4]. In the last 5–10 years, there has been a marked uptick in the use of ARTs for family building by same-sex couples [5]. When the *Obergefell v. Hodges* Supreme Court ruling legalized same-sex marriage in 2015, instances of same-sex marriage more than doubled [5]. Research conducted prior to that decision demonstrated that married same-sex couples were twice as likely to have children than their unmarried counterparts [6, 7]. Of the 4.5% of the US population that identifies as LGBT, 29% are currently raising children [8]. In addition to those living with LGBT parent(s), a significant number of children are currently living in households with only one parent; 23% of children in the U.S. are living with a single mother, and 4% are living with a single father. 4% of children are living with both parents who are not married to one another and 3.8% of children do not live with either parent [9].

Despite the recent increase in nontraditional family structures, there is still a certain degree of controversy over the provision of fertility services to LGBT individuals. Fertility clinics across the country vary in the services they are willing to provide to DSG persons [5]. Surveys of fertility clinics in the United States found that at least some proportion of programs would turn away LGBT and unmarried individuals [10, 11]. In a study that surveyed U.S. fertility clinic websites for LGBT-specific content to assess geographical distribution and practice characteristics of clinics inclusive of LGBT patients, Wu et al. found that over half of Society for Assisted Reproductive Technology (SART) clinics included LGBT content. Clinics in the Midwest and South were significantly less likely to do so [5].

Ethical Considerations

Autonomy: Reproductive Interests

Studies have shown that individuals – regardless of sexual orientation, marital status or gender identity – may desire to have biologically related children and to raise them, alone or with a partner [9]. In 2019, the nonprofit group "Family Equality" conducted a survey of LGBTQ people in the United States to ascertain interest in and plans for family building. The survey found that 63% of LGBTQ millennials (aged 18–35) are considering expanding their families by either having children for the first time or by having more children [12]. They also found that 48% of LGBTQ millennials are actively planning to build families, compared to 55% of non-LGBTQ millennials [12]. This gap has narrowed significantly compared to older generations. Several studies, which have focused specifically on the transgender population, have found that family-building is valued by many transgender persons [13–15].

Individuals desire children for a variety of reasons: they may want to create a sense of family with a partner and a child, they may hope for future grandchildren, or they may want loved ones to care for them when they are elderly. These are core human values, and they should be respected without discrimination based on marital status, sexual orientation or gender identity [9]. There is no sound basis that marital status, sexual orientation or gender identity impact interests in reproduction [9].

Most single and diverse sexuality and gender (DSG) individuals and couples cannot biologically reproduce on their own [9]. Assisted reproductive technologies can be utilized by individuals and couples who wish to have children; some examples include:

– Single women: intrauterine insemination (IUI) with donor sperm
– Single males and same-sex male couples: IVF with donor eggs, followed by embryo transfer to gestational carrier
– Same-sex female couples: one partner undergoes IUI and carries the child to term or one partner provides oocytes for IVF using donor sperm, and the resulting embryo is transferred to the other partner
– Transgender individuals who intend to undergo gender-affirming care: fertility preservation (e.g., sperm, oocyte, embryo or ovarian tissue cryopreservation) prior gender transition; assisted reproduction may then include the full range of fertility services and does not differ significantly from services offered to nontransgender individuals (see more extensive discussion of assisted reproduction and transgender persons in chapter "Medically Assisted Reproduction and Transgender Persons") [16]
– Non-binary, agender, or transgender individuals who have not had/do not plan to have medical gender-affirming procedures: assisted reproduction may include the full spectrum of fertility services offered to cisgender people

It is important to note that these generalized categories often overlap and cannot be sharply distinguished [17].

When faced with physiological constraints to reproduction, individuals may seek out nonmedical forms of assisted reproduction, which involve both medical and legal risks [18]. For example, if one utilizes sperm from a donor who provided gametes in a manner not legally protected by state law, the sperm donor may be judged to be the legal father of children conceived using their sperm, in an outcome desired neither by the donor nor the intended parent [9]. Utilizing donor sperm without medical screening also poses risks of exposure to genetic or sexually-transmitted diseases. When donors or gestational carriers are family members or friends, issues arise around informed consent. Therefore, it is critical that any individual or couple pursuing family building via assisted reproduction seek out infertility care and legal advice so that they can be counseled on all available family-building options, recommended medical screening and legal protections [9].

Justice

The principle of justice posits that similar cases should be treated similarly. Different treatment is only justified if there is a *morally relevant* difference between cases [17]. In this case, there is no evidence that marital status, gender identity or sexual orientation impact the ability to parent [9]. Since the state does not restrict the reproductive autonomy of adults who can conceive without assistance, the selective interference in the reproductive autonomy of those who rely on ART to conceive is unjust and discriminatory [19]. According to the ASRM, "program policies regarding access to care should be consistent across patients irrespective of marital status, sexual orientation or gender identity." [9].

Right to Reproduce

When considering the right to reproduce, there are negative and positive rights. The negative right is the right to be free from interference should one want to conceive; in other words, this is the right to bodily integrity and to be free from forced sterilization [17]. The positive right to reproduce is the right to get help from others (i.e., medically-assisted reproduction and fertility preservation) to reproduce [17]. Though the right of people to reproduce without regard to marital status, sexual orientation or gender identity is becoming increasingly accepted, there are parts of the U.S. and the world where it is contested [17]. Some objections are consequentialist, highlighting the risks to resulting children and to society; this objection will be discussed in the "Welfare of the Child" section below [17]. Others are deontological, claiming that alternative family structures are unnatural and that their creation is at odds with the goals of medicine [17]. The presumed conflict between the goals of medicine and the use of ARTs for unmarried and DSG persons is problematic. If one regards the goals of medicine as simply to prevent and cure disease, ARTs would only be used to treat infertility and subfertility [17]. However, many widely accepted medical practices address goals beyond preventing and curing disease. Examples include medical treatment during pregnancy, sterilization, and cosmetic surgery. "Health" and "disease" are far from objective categories [17]. The argument that ARTs should not be offered to unmarried and DSG persons because it is "unnatural" is also flawed. This argument can only succeed if "there is an interpretation of the term '(un)natural' which enables us both to distinguish between natural and unnatural conditions/ actions and to understand what there is about the latter which is morally objectionable. It is doubtful as to whether there is any such interpretation which is convincing." [20].

Welfare of the Child

Individuals may greatly benefit from having children through the use of assisted reproductive technologies. However, there is some debate about whether growing up in an alternative family structure will pose psychosocial risks to children [17]. Can clinicians limit reproductive autonomy due to concerns about parental "fitness"?

A number of studies, mostly pre-dating *Obergefell vs. Hodges,* have investigated the welfare of children in nontraditional families. In 2004, the American Psychological Association reviewed existing data and found that there was no evidence that parenting effectiveness was related to parental sexual orientation or gender identity [21]. In their opinion on provision of fertility treatment to DSG individuals and couples, the ASRM Ethics Committee summarized more research on the topic, which continued to show that sexual orientation of parent(s) does not adversely impact offspring [9]. For example, a Dutch study found no significant differences in the rate of problem behaviors in adolescents born from lesbian parents versus cisgender heterosexual parents [22]. Other studies have found that children in adoptive families had no differences in adjustment based on parental sexual orientation [23, 24]. A study of adults raised in the U.S. by lesbian and gay parents reported some differences in childhood experiences but not in adjustment in adulthood [25]. The European Society of Human Reproduction and Embryology (ESHRE) reported that studies on single women opting for donor insemination revealed that these women were by and large psychologically healthy and had social networks to support them during the child-rearing process [17].

Overall, research supports the notion that the quality of family relationships is more impactful on a child's development than the way in which a family is formed [17]. Divorce is arguably more challenging for children to cope with than the non-traditional nature of their family structure. Do clinicians also have an obligation to ensure that intended parents who are married to one another do not get divorced after they have a child?

Professional Autonomy

Those who do not require fertility treatment determine whether or not to have children privately. Those who require medical assistance necessarily implicate physicians in their fertility process. Are physicians obligated to treat any patient who requests treatment?

Resistance to treat unmarried or DSG persons might be due to the administrative challenges of working with gamete donors and gestational carriers [9]. It might also be rooted in the religious beliefs that regard reproduction outside of heterosexual marriage as morally questionable [9]. While physician autonomy is an important value, the ASRM correctly states that "services provided by fertility clinics should be consistent across patients irrespective of marital status, sexual orientation or gender identity." [9] Some states have antidiscrimination laws prohibiting fertility clinics from denying patients services based on their sexual orientation, even if the refusal is based on religious views [9].

Conclusion

Research clearly indicates that marital status, gender identity and sexual orientation do not impact parenting ability. As a result, requests to build families with ARTs should be considered without regard to these factors, and should only be refused if there is a "substantial, non-arbitrary bias" for believing that the patient would provide inadequate or unsafe child-rearing [26]. Such a conclusion should only be made after a thorough review performed by a multidisciplinary treatment team.

The ASRM Ethics Committee believes in the ethical duty to treat single individuals, unmarried couples and DSG individuals and couples "in the same manner as cisgender heterosexual married couples in determining which services to provide [9]. ESHRE has also concluded "that the categorical denial of these services cannot be reconciled with a human rights perspective" [17].

Works Cited

1. Roberts DE. Race, Gender, and Genetic Technologies: A New Reproductive Dystopia? *Signs J Women Cult Soc.* 2009;34(4):783–804. https://doi.org/10.1086/597132
2. Lewin E. On the Outside Looking In: The Politics of Lesbian Motherhood.". In: *Conceiving the New World Order: The Global Politics of Reproduction.* University of California Press; 1995:103–121.
3. Smietana M, Thompson C, Twine FW. Making and breaking families – reading queer reproductions, stratified reproduction and reproductive justice together. *Reprod Biomed Soc Online.* 2018;7:112–130. https://doi.org/10.1016/j.rbms.2018.11.001
4. Disparities in access to effective treatment for infertility in the United States: an Ethics Committee opinion. *Fertil Steril.* 2021;116(1):54–63. https://doi.org/10.1016/j.fertnstert.2021.02.019
5. Wu HY, Yin O, Monseur B, et al. Lesbian, gay, bisexual, transgender content on reproductive endocrinology and infertility clinic websites. *Fertil Steril.* 2017;108(1):183–191. https://doi.org/10.1016/j.fertnstert.2017.05.011
6. Gates: Marriage and same-sex couples after Obergefell – Google Scholar. Accessed July 4, 2022. https://scholar.google.com/scholar_lookup?title=Marriage%20and%20same-sex%20couples%20after%20Obergefel&author=G.%20Gates&publication_year=2015
7. Gates: Demographics of married and unmarried same-sex... - Google Scholar. Accessed July 4, 2022. https://scholar.google.com/scholar_lookup?title=Demographics%20of%20married%20and%20unmarried%20same-sex%20couples%3A%20analyses%20of%20the%202013%20American%20Community%20Survey&author=G.%20Gates&publication_year=2015
8. LGBT Data & Demographics – The Williams Institute. Accessed July 4, 2022. https://williamsinstitute.law.ucla.edu/visualization/lgbt-stats/?topic=LGBT#demographic
9. Ethics Committee of the American Society for Reproductive Medicine. Access to fertility treatment irrespective of marital status, sexual orientation, or gender identity: an Ethics Committee opinion. *Fertil Steril.* 2021;116(2):326–330. https://doi.org/10.1016/j.fertnstert.2021.03.034
10. Gurmankin AD, Caplan AL, Braverman AM. Screening practices and beliefs of assisted reproductive technology programs. *Fertil Steril.* 2005;83(1):61–67. https://doi.org/10.1016/j.fertnstert.2004.06.048
11. Lawrence RE, Rasinski KA, Yoon JD, Curlin FA. Obstetrician–Gynecologists' Beliefs About Assisted Reproductive Technologies. *Obstet Gynecol.* 2010;116(1):127–135. https://doi.org/10.1097/AOG.0b013e3181e2f27d
12. Family Equality | LGBTQ Family Building Survey. Family Equality. Accessed July 6, 2022. https://www.familyequality.org/resources/lgbtq-family-building-survey/
13. Auer MK, Fuss J, Nieder TO, et al. Desire to Have Children Among Transgender People in Germany: A Cross-Sectional Multi-Center Study. *J Sex Med.* 2018;15(5):757–767. https://doi.org/10.1016/j.jsxm.2018.03.083

14. von Doussa H, Power J, Riggs D. Imagining parenthood: the possibilities and experiences of parenthood among transgender people. *Cult Health Sex.* 2015;17(9):1119–1131. https://doi.org/10.1080/13691058.2015.1042919
15. Tornello SL, Bos H. Parenting Intentions Among Transgender Individuals. *LGBT Health.* 2017;4(2):115–120. https://doi.org/10.1089/lgbt.2016.0153
16. Access to fertility services by transgender and nonbinary persons: an Ethics Committee opinion. *Fertil Steril.* 2021;115(4):874–878. https://doi.org/10.1016/j.fertnstert.2021.01.049
17. De Wert G, Dondorp W, Shenfield F, et al. ESHRE Task Force on Ethics and Law 23: medically assisted reproduction in singles, lesbian and gay couples, and transsexual people†. *Hum Reprod Oxf Engl.* 2014;29(9):1859–1865. https://doi.org/10.1093/humrep/deu183
18. Provision of fertility services for women at increased risk of complications during fertility treatment or pregnancy: an Ethics Committee opinion. *Fertil Steril.* 2022;117(4):713–719. https://doi.org/10.1016/j.fertnstert.2021.12.030
19. Jackson E. *Regulating Reproduction: Law, Technology and Autonomy.* Hart Publishing; 2001.
20. Warren MA. *Gendercide.* UK ed. edition. Rowman & Allanfield Publishers; 1985.
21. American Psychological Association Resolution on Sexual Orientation, Parents and Children. Published online 2004.
22. van Rijn-van Gelderen L, Bos HMW, Gartrell NK. Dutch adolescents from lesbian-parent families: How do they compare to peers with heterosexual parents and what is the impact of homophobic stigmatization? *J Adolesc.* 2015;40:65–73. https://doi.org/10.1016/j.adolescence.2015.01.005
23. Farr RH. Does parental sexual orientation matter? A longitudinal follow-up of adoptive families with school-age children. *Dev Psychol.* 2017;53(2):252–264. https://doi.org/10.1037/dev0000228
24. Goldberg AE, Smith JZ. Predictors of psychological adjustment in early placed adopted children with lesbian, gay, and heterosexual parents. *J Fam Psychol.* 2013;27(3):431–442. https://doi.org/10.1037/a0032911
25. Lick DJ, Patterson CJ, Schmidt KM. Recalled Social Experiences and Current Psychological Adjustment among Adults Reared by Gay and Lesbian Parents. *J GLBT Fam Stud.* 2013;9(3):230–253. https://doi.org/10.1080/1550428X.2013.781907
26. Child-rearing ability and the provision of fertility services: a committee opinion. *Fertil Steril.* 2013;100(1):50–53. https://doi.org/10.1016/j.fertnstert.2013.02.023

Medically Assisted Reproduction and Transgender Persons

Paula Amato

Abstract Requests for assisted reproduction by transgender persons appear to be increasing. This chapter outlines relevant ethical considerations (autonomy, reproductive rights, child welfare, and non-discrimination) and provides guidance to clinicians regarding requests for medically assisted reproduction and fertility preservation for transgender persons. Those who advocate for inclusive access to fertility services note that transgender persons often express the desire to have children and should be afforded the human right of an opportunity to procreate. Cryopreservation of gametes or embryos is a viable option for assisted reproduction in transgender patients, however, knowledge about both the impact of long-term hormone therapy on gametogenesis and the recovery of reproductive function after stopping pubertal blockers and cross-hormone therapy is limited. Professional autonomy in deciding whom to treat is also limited by an obligation to consider all patients equally regardless of gender identity (non-discrimination). Those who oppose access to ART by transgender people do so out of concern for well-being of future children (beneficence/non-maleficence), though this concern is not supported by research results (Freedman, Clin Child Psychol Psychiatry 7:42, 2002; White and Ettner, J Gay Lesbian Psychother 8:129–145, 2008; Green, Int J Transgenderism 2:4, 1998). There is no ethical basis to deny transgender people access to assisted reproduction. Resources should continue to be allocated towards creating culturally sensitive educational materials, training providers to provide competent care for transgender patients and continuing to research fertility preservation and long-term outcomes of hormone therapy.

Keywords LGBTQ+ · Transgender · Cryopreservation · Hormone therapy · Autonomy

P. Amato (✉)
Department of Obstetrics & Gynecology, Division of Reproductive Endocrinology & Infertility, Oregon Health & Science University, Portland, OR, USA

© The Author(s), under exclusive license to Springer Nature Switzerland AG 2023
L. P. King, I. C. Band (eds.), *Case Studies in the Ethics of Assisted Reproduction*, https://doi.org/10.1007/978-3-031-41215-8_13

Case

A female-to-male (FTM) 30-year-old and his cisgender female partner present for fertility counseling. The patient initiated transition with hormones three years prior, but wants to temporarily discontinue testosterone use in order to try to get pregnant and carry a child. Due to the patient's three years of testosterone exposure, he suspects that he will require assistance of a fertility specialist to conceive. Long-term exogenous hormone use may be associated with a number of health risks. However, whether long-term hormone exposure confers any unique medical risk to a patient undergoing ART procedures or any long-term impact on gametes and fertility is unknown.

Scope of the Question

Requests for medically assisted reproduction by transgender persons appear to be increasing. This chapter aims to elucidate the ethical considerations and provide guidance to clinicians regarding requests for medically assisted reproduction and fertility preservation for transgender persons. Issues concerning fertility preservation in prepubertal children are beyond the scope of this chapter.[1] Although we refer to binary definitions of gender for the sake of simplicity, we recognize that gender is a continuum and the issues discussed herein apply equally to non-binary individuals as well.

Background

Gender dysphoria is characterized by persistent incongruence between an experienced gender and the assigned sex of an individual at birth. This often causes emotional distress (American Psychiatric Association, 2013). Gender-affirming treatment has been shown to decrease the psychological suffering and psychiatric morbidity of transgender persons (WPATH, 2011). While many transgender persons desire to start hormonal therapy followed by gender-affirming surgery, not all do so.

In the U.S., 0.3–2% of the population identify as transgender (Flores et al., 2016). The World Professional Association of Transgender Health (WPATH) estimates the prevalence for male-to-female individuals is 1:45,000 to 1:12,000, and for female-to-male individuals is 1:200,000 to 1:30,400 (Hunger, 2012). The American Psychological Association, American Psychiatry Association, and WPATH have all

---

[1] Editor's note: See "Further Reading" section at end of the chapter for more on prepubertal fertility preservation.

concluded that gender dysphoria by itself does not constitute a psychiatric disorder (APA, 2008, 2013; WPATH, 2011).

Transgender persons often have the same family-building interests as cisgender persons; surveys show that many transgender persons are of reproductive age at the time of transition and desire eventual childbearing (Wierckx et al., 2012). However, cross-hormone therapy and gender-affirming surgery may compromise fertility. WPATH and the Endocrine Society recommend that transgender persons be counseled about the effect of transition on their fertility and informed of their fertility preservation and reproductive options ideally before initiating transition (Hembree et al., 2009; WPATH, 2011). These options typically include gamete preservation whether oocyte or sperm.

Transgender persons have historically faced barriers to access to fertility services. Resistance is usually based on concerns for the welfare of future children. It has been increasingly argued that transgender persons should have access to fertility services (ASRM, 2015; DeWert et al., 2014). Requests for treatment by transgender individuals raise questions about autonomy, reproductive rights, child welfare, and non-discrimination.

Ethical Considerations

Autonomy

"The human right to maintain personal bodily autonomy, have children, not have children, and parent the children we have in safe and sustainable communities," is a cornerstone of reproductive justice (Sister Song, 2022). Recent studies show that many transgender persons wish to have children and to gestate a pregnancy. A Belgian study in 2012 found that more than half (54%) of surveyed transgender men desired to have children, and more than one third (37%) would have considered freezing oocytes if that option had been available (Wierckx et al., 2012). A German study found that 76% of both transgender men and women had thought about fertility preservation before transition, but only 9% of transgender women and 3% of transgender men had completed the process (Auer et al., 2018). Data regarding the counseling and access afforded these persons was not available.

The right to decide the number and spacing of children was formally recognized by the Proclamation of Tehran at the United Nations 1968 International Conference on Human Rights (United Nations, 1968). Based on these principles, the same rights to sexual and reproductive health should be guaranteed to transgender persons (ASRM, 2015; De Wert et al., 2014).

Beneficence and Non-maleficence

Exogenous hormone therapy and gonadectomy have recognized impacts on fertility. Reproduction in transgender persons who have already initiated transition will usually involve discontinuation of exogenous hormones, which can be associated with worsening gender dysphoria. Providers should offer psychological counseling and support by a qualified mental health professional.

In trans women, gonadectomy results in permanent effects on fertility and estrogen therapy results in impaired spermatogenesis, though little is known about the long-term effects of estrogen on testicular function and morphology. Most data show impaired spermatogenesis and morphological changes (Jindarak et al., 2018; Kent et al., 2018; Leavy et al., 2017; Schneider et al., 2015; Jiang et al., 2019). Whether treatment duration is an important factor to consider is unknown. Similarly, our knowledge is limited concerning the potential for reversibility of the effects of estrogen on testicular function after treatment cessation. The optimal interval between the cessation of gender-affirming treatment and the timing of fertility preservation remains to be determined. Further research is warranted to optimize outcomes and counseling.

Post pubertal trans women can undergo sperm cryopreservation or testicular tissue cryopreservation. The sperm can then be used to inseminate a female partner or for in-vitro fertilization. Testicular tissue cryopreservation in prepubertal children is still considered experimental. Although uterine transplantation has been successfully performed and resulted in several live births worldwide, all the cases thus far have been performed in cisgender women (Jones et al., 2019) and plans for research in this area have typically argued that trans persons should be excluded for a variety of reasons (Lefkowitz, 2012). The ethics of these exclusions and of uterine transplantation in general are beyond the scope of this chapter and are actively being investigated.

In trans men, gonadectomy causes permanent, irreversible effects on fertility. Testosterone therapy can impact fertility and usually causes amenorrhea. Chronic administration of testosterone leads to morphological changes in the ovaries (Pache et al., 1991; Ikeda et al., 2013; Grynberg et al., 2010; De Roo et al., 2017). It remains unresolved whether effects of androgens on ovarian morphology and function are reversible. Few studies have examined the effects of androgen exposure on the uterus (Loverro et al., 2016; Grimstad et al., 2019).

The options for fertility preservation in trans men include oocyte and embryo cryopreservation. Ovarian tissue cryopreservation is considered experimental. Novel methods such as in-vitro maturation of gametes are under development and may hold promise for the future. Oocyte or embryo cryopreservation involves ovarian stimulation and oocyte retrieval. Usually, trans men are advised to stop their testosterone therapy for a period of time (3–6 months) at least until menses return. The oocytes can later be fertilized with partner or donor sperm and the embryo transferred into a partner's or gestational carrier's uterus.

A recent study by Leung et al investigated assisted reproductive technology (ART) outcomes in female-to-male transgender patients compared to a matched cisgender cohort. The study concluded that ART outcomes are similar even in patients who had already initiated testosterone therapy (Leung et al., 2019). Whether long-term hormone exposure confers any unique medical risks to the patient undergoing assisted reproduction procedures or has any long-term impact on gametes and/or offspring is currently unknown.

Our current knowledge is limited regarding the recovery of reproductive function after stopping pubertal blockers and cross-hormone therapy in transgender youth. Fertility preservation should be discussed with transgender youth before pubertal suppression. Techniques for the in-vitro maturation of immature germ cells are still experimental (Yin et al., 2016; Abir et al., 2016; Segers et al., 2015). There may be additional ethical considerations for children and adolescents on pubertal suppression therapy who desire fertility preservation, which are beyond the scope of this chapter.

Transgender persons typically desire to have children, create families, and assume parental roles in a manner reaffirming their gender identity. Successful pregnancies have been reported in transgender men previously treated with testosterone (Light et al., 2014). Functional lactation was successfully induced using the dopamine antagonist (domperidone) in a transgender woman desiring to breastfeed (Reisman and Goldstein, 2018).

Further research is needed to provide evidence-based and patient-centered care and to understand the medical and psychosocial risks and impacts for parents and offspring during treatment, the perinatal period, and on future health.

Outcomes for Children Raised by Transgender Parents

Many who oppose reproduction by transgender persons do so out of concern for the well-being of the children (Golombok, 1998). Although research and data are scarce, the available data suggests that transgender identity of a parent does not have a negative impact on the psychosexual development of the children (Freedman et al., 2002; White and Ettner, 2008; Green, 1998).

A recent study in France included 42 children conceived by donor insemination to transgender men. The study concluded that the children are healthy, well-adjusted, and show secure attachment to their parents (Chiland et al., 2013). Thus, the available data do not support the fear that being raised by a transgender parent will necessarily result in poor outcomes (American Academy of Child & Adolescent Psychiatry, 2019; Stotzer et al., 2014). The American Academy of Child and Adolescent Psychiatry affirms that there is no evidence to support that parents who are transgender are deficient in parenting skills, child-centered concerns, and parent-child attachments compared with cisgender parents (American Academy of Child & Adolescent Psychiatry, 2019).

Furthermore, the ASRM and its Ethics Committee statement on Child-rearing Ability and the Provision of Fertility Services, warns that it is difficult to make accurate predictions about parental child-rearing for any prospective parents and health care professionals should avoid attempting to make them (ASRM, 2017).

Justice

Transgender people experience social and health disparities, including social harassment and discrimination, abandonment by family or friends, and poor access to health care (Factor and Rothblum, 2007; Grant et al., 2011; James et al., 2016). Transgender people also experience barriers to accessing medically assisted reproduction and fertility preservation services (Tishelman, 2019), however the American Medical Association (AMA) and the American College of Obstetricians and Gynecologists (ACOG) both oppose discrimination based on gender identify (AMA, 2010; ACOG, 2011a, b).

Utilization of fertility preservation in transgender people is low overall and is more frequent among transgender females than transgender males (Riggs and Bartholomaeus, 2018; Nahata et al., 2017; Chen et al., 2017). Among the identified barriers to fertility preservation are cost, lack of information, invasiveness of procedures, and desire not to delay medical transition. The cost of fertility preservation and medically assisted reproduction services can be prohibitive. Costs are especially significant for egg freezing and in-vitro fertilization.

Several states have anti-discrimination laws that provide express protections for transgender persons (National Center for Lesbian Rights, 2010). Denial of treatment based solely on gender identify thus may be prohibited discrimination in some jurisdictions. Providers should encourage transgender patients to consult appropriate professionals to become informed about the legal issues involved in becoming a parent through ART.

Conclusions

Gender-affirming treatment, together with psychosocial and medical care has been found to alleviate psychological distress in this population. In addition, transgender people often express the desire to have children and to create families. Based on ethical principles, these individuals should have the same rights as cisgender persons to benefit from fertility preservation and assisted reproduction. The Endocrine Society and WPATH both recommend that health care professionals provide information for fertility risk and fertility preservation ideally before transition.

Ethicists have concluded that there is no ethical basis to deny transgender individuals access to reproductive medicine. Both the American Society for Reproductive Medicine (ASRM) and European Society of Human Reproduction and Embryology

(ESHRE) have issued opinions that transgender patients should have the same access to fertility options as cisgender patients (ASRM, 2015; De Wert et al., 2014).

Professional autonomy in deciding whom to treat is limited in this case by a greater ethical obligation, and in some jurisdictions, a legal duty, to regard all persons equally, regardless of their gender identity. Programs without sufficient resources to care for transgender patients have an ethical duty to refer to health care professionals equipped to treat such patients.

Current challenges include lack of culturally sensitive educational materials, insufficient training of health care professionals, lack of established methods for fertility preservation in prepubertal youth and lack of data on long-term outcomes in this population. A multidisciplinary approach is recommended. Further studies are needed to be able to provide evidence-based counseling.

Works Cited/Further Reading

Abir R, Ben-Aharon I, Garor R, Yaniv I, Ash S, Stemmer SM, et al. Cryopreservation of in vitro matured oocytes in addition to ovarian tissue freezing for fertility preservation in paediatric female cancer patients before and after cancer therapy. Hum Reprod. 2016;31(4):750–62.

American Academy of Child & Adolescent Psychiatry. (2019, May). *Gay, lesbian, bisexual, or transgender parents*. https://www.aacap.org/

American College of Obstetricians and Gynecologists. Code of professional ethics. (Last accessed May, 2020) ACOG, Washington, DC; 2011a http://www.acog.org/-/media/Departments/National-Officer-Nominations-Process/ACOGcode.pdf

American College of Obstetricians and Gynecologists. Health Care for Transgender Individuals. Committee Opinion No 512. *Obstet Gynecol*. 2011b; 118: 1454–1458

American Medical Association. AMA Policies on LGBT Issues. (Last accessed May, 2020); 2010 http://www.ama-assn.org//ama/pub/about-ama/our-people/member-groups-sections/glbt-advisory-committee/ama-policy-regarding-sexual-orientation.page

American Psychiatric Association. Diagnostic and Statistical Manual of Mental Disorders. 5th Ed. Arlington, VA: American Psychiatric Publishing; 2013.

APA Task Force on Gender Identity and Gender Variance. Report of the Task Force on Gender Identity and Gender Variance. (Last accessed May 20, 2020) American Psychological Association, Washington DC; 2008

Auer, M. K., Fuss, J., Nieder, T. O., Briken, P., Biedermann, S. V., Stalla, G. K., . . . Hildebrandt, T. (2018). Desire to Have Children Among Transgender People in Germany: A Cross-Sectional Multi-Center Study. *J Sex Med, 15*(5), 757–767.

Chen, D., Simons, L., Johnson, E. K., Lockart, B. A., & Finlayson, C. (2017). Fertility Preservation for Transgender Adolescents. *J Adolesc Health, 61*(1), 120–123.

Chiland C, Clouet AM, Golse B, Guinot M, Wolf JP. A new type of family: Transmen as fathers thanks to donor sperm insemination. A 12-year follow-up exploratory study of their children. Neuropsychiatrie de l'Enfance et de l'Adolescence, Volume 61, Issue 6, 2013.

De Roo, C., Lierman, S., Tilleman, K., Peynshaert, K., Braeckmans, K., Caanen, M., . . . De Sutter, P. (2017). Ovarian tissue cryopreservation in female-to-male transgender people: insights into ovarian histology and physiology after prolonged androgen treatment. *Reprod Biomed Online, 34*(6), 557–566.

De Wert G, Dondorp W, Shenfield F, Barri P, Devroey P, Diedrich K, Tarlatzis B, Provoost V, Pennings G. ESHRE Task Force on Ethics and Law 23: medically assisted reproduction in singles, lesbian and gay couples, and transsexual people†. Hum Reprod. 2014 Sep;29(9):1859–65. https://doi.org/10.1093/humrep/deu183. Epub 2014 Jul 22. PubMed PMID: 25052011.

Ethics Committee of the American Society for Reproductive Medicine. Access to fertility services by transgender persons: an Ethics Committee opinion. *Fertil Steril.* 2015;104(5):1111–1115. https://doi.org/10.1016/j.fertnstert.2015.08.021

Ethics Committee of the American Society for Reproductive Medicine. Electronic address: ASRM@asrm.org; Ethics Committee of the American Society for Reproductive Medicine. Child-rearing ability and the provision of fertility services: an Ethics Committee opinion. *Fertil Steril.* 2017;108(6):944–947. https://doi.org/10.1016/j.fertnstert.2017.10.006

Factor, R. J., & Rothblum, E. D. (2007). A study of transgender adults and their non-transgender siblings on demographic characteristics, social support, and experiences of violence. *J LGBT Health Res, 3*(3), 11–30.

Flores AR, Herman JL, Gates GJ, Brown TNT. How many adults identify as transgender in the United States. Williams Institute; 2016. Available at: https://williamsinstitute.law.ucla.edu/research/how-many-adults-identifyas-transgender-in-the-united-states/. Accessed May, 2020.

Freedman, D., Tasker, F., and Di Ceglie, D. Transsexual Parents Referred to a Specialist Gender Identity Development Service: A Brief Report of Key Developmental Features. *Clin Child Psychol Psychiatry.* 2002; 7: 423

Golombok, S. New Families, old values: considerations regarding the welfare of the child. *Hum Reprod.* 1998; 3: 2342–2347

Grant, J. E., Flynn, M., Odlaug, B. L., & Schreiber, L. R. (2011). Personality disorders in gay, lesbian, bisexual, and transgender chemically dependent patients. *Am J Addict, 20*(5), 405–411.

Green, R. Transsexuals' Children. (Last accessed May, 2020) *The international journal of transgenderism.* 1998; 2: 4 http://www.iiav.nl/ezines/web/IJT/97-03/numbers/symposion/ijtc0601.html

Grimstad, F. W., Fowler, K. G., New, E. P., Ferrando, C. A., Pollard, R. R., Chapman, G., . . . Gray, M. (2019). Uterine pathology in transmasculine persons on testosterone: a retrospective multicenter case series. *Am J Obstet Gynecol, 220*(3), 257.e251–257.e257.

Grynberg M, Fanchin R, Dubost G, et al. Histology of genital tract and breast tissue after long-term testosterone administration in a female-to-male transsexual population. *Reprod Biomed Online.* 2010; 20: 553–558.

Hembree WC, Cohen-Kettenis P, Delemarre-van de Waal HA, et al. Endocrine treatment of transsexual persons: an Endocrine Society clinical practice guideline. *J Clin Endocrinol Metab.* 2009;94: 3132– 3154.

Hunger S. Commentary: Transgender people are not that different after all. Camb Q Healthc Ethics 2012;21:287–9.

Ikeda K, Baba T, Noguchi H, Nagasawa K, Endo T, Kiya T, et al. Excessive androgen exposure in female-to-male transsexual persons of reproductive age induces hyperplasia of the ovarian cortex and stroma but not polycystic ovary morphology. Hum Reprod 2013;28:453–61.

James SE, Rankin H, Keis-ling M, Mottet L, Anafi M. The Report of the 2015 U.S. Transgender Survey. Washington, DC: National Center for Transgender Equality; 2016.

Jiang, D. D., Swenson, E., Mason, M., Turner, K. R., Dugi, D. D., Hedges, J. C., & Hecht, S. L. (2019). Effects of Estrogen on Spermatogenesis in Transgender Women. *Urology, 132,* 117–122.

Jindarak S, Nilprapha K, Atikankul T, et al. Spermatogenesis abnormalities following hormonal therapy in transwomen. *Biomed Res Int.* 2018; 2018: 7919481

Jones, B. P., Williams, N. J., Saso, S., Thum, M. Y., Quiroga, I., Yazbek, J., . . . Smith, J. R. (2019). Uterine transplantation in transgender women. *Bjog, 126*(2), 152–156.

Kent, M. A., Winoker, J. S., & Grotas, A. B. (2018). Effects of Feminizing Hormones on Sperm Production and Malignant Changes: Microscopic Examination of Post Orchiectomy Specimens in Transwomen. *Urology, 121,* 93–96.

Leavy M, Trottmann M, Liedl B, et al. Effects of Elevated beta-estradiol levels on the functional morphology of the testis – new insights. *Sci Rep.* 2017; 7: 39931.

Lefkowitz. (2012). https://pubmed.ncbi.nlm.nih.gov/22356169/

Leung, A., Sakkas, D., Pang, S., Thornton, K., & Resetkova, N. (2019). Assisted reproductive technology outcomes in female-to-male transgender patients compared with cisgender patients: a new frontier in reproductive medicine. *Fertil Steril, 112*(5), 858–865.

Light, A. D., Obedin-Maliver, J., Sevelius, J. M., & Kerns, J. L. (2014). Transgender men who experienced pregnancy after female-to-male gender transitioning. *Obstet Gynecol, 124*(6), 1120–1127.

Loverro, G., Resta, L., Dellino, M., Edoardo, D. N., Cascarano, M. A., Loverro, M., & Mastrolia, S. A. (2016). Uterine and ovarian changes during testosterone administration in young female-to-male transsexuals. *Taiwan J Obstet Gynecol, 55*(5), 686–691.

Nahata, L., Tishelman, A. C., Caltabellotta, N. M., & Quinn, G. P. (2017). Low Fertility Preservation Utilization Among Transgender Youth. *J Adolesc Health, 61*(1), 40–44.

National Center for Lesbian Rights. State by state guide to laws that prohibit discrimination against transgender people. (Available at:) (Last accessed May, 2020); 2010 http://www.lgbtagingcenter.org/resources/pdfs/StateLawsThatProhibitDiscriminationAgainstTransPeople.pdf

Pache TD, Chadha S, Gooren LJ, et al. Ovarian morphology in long-term androgen-treated female to male transsexuals. A human model for the study of polycystic ovarian syndrome? *Histopathology*. 1991; 19: 445–452.

Proclamation of Teheran, Final Act of the International Conference on Human Rights, Teheran, 22 April to 13 May 1968, U.N. Doc. A/CONF. 32/41 at 3; 1968.

Reisman, T., & Goldstein, Z. (2018). Case Report: Induced Lactation in a Transgender Woman. *Transgend Health, 3*(1), 24–26.

Riggs, D. W., & Bartholomaeus, C. (2018). Fertility preservation decision making amongst Australian transgender and non-binary adults. *Reprod Health, 15*(1), 181.

Schneider, F., Neuhaus, N., Wistuba, J., Zitzmann, M., Heß, J., Mahler, D., . . . Kliesch, S. (2015). Testicular Functions and Clinical Characterization of Patients with Gender Dysphoria (GD) Undergoing Sex Reassignment Surgery (SRS). *J Sex Med, 12*(11), 2190–2200.

Segers I, Mateizel I, Van Moer E, Smitz J, Tournaye H, Verheyen G, et al. In vitro maturation (IVM) of oocytes recovered from ovariectomy specimens in the laboratory: a promising "ex vivo" method of oocyte cryopreservation resulting in the first report of an ongoing pregnancy in Europe. J Assist Reprod Genet. 2015;32(8):1221–31.

Sister Song. Reproductive Justice. Accessed July 14, 2022. https://www.sistersong.net/reproductive-justice

Stotzer, R. L, Herman, J. L, & Hasenbush, A. (2014). Transgender Parenting: A Review of Existing Research. *UCLA: The Williams Institute*. Retrieved May, 2020 from https://escholarship.org/uc/item/3rp0v7qv

Tishelman AC, Sutter ME, Chen D, et al. Health care provider perceptions of fertility preservation barriers and challenges with transgender patients and families: qualitative responses to an international survey. J Assist Reprod Genet. 2019;36(3):579–588. https://doi.org/10.1007/s10815-018-1395-y

White, T. and Ettner, R. Disclosure, Risk and Protective Factors for Children Whose Parents Are Undergoing a Gender Transition. *J Gay Lesbian Psychother*. 2008; 8: 129–145

Wierckx K, Van Caenegem E, Pennings G, Elaut E, Dedecker D, Van de Peer F, Weyers S, De Sutter P, T'Sjoen G. Reproductive wish in transsexual men. Hum Reprod. 2012 Feb;27(2):483–7.

World Professional Association for Transgender Health. Standards of Care. Version 7. https://www.wpath.org. 2011 Retrieved May, 2020.

Yin H, Jiang H, Kristensen SG, Andersen CY. Vitrification of in vitro matured oocytes collected from surplus ovarian medulla tissue resulting from fertility preservation of ovarian cortex tissue. J Assist Reprod Genet. 2016;33(6):741–6.

Further Reading on Prepubertal Fertility Preservation

McDougall RJ, Gillam L, Delany C, et al. Ethics of fertility preservation for prepubertal children: should clinicians offer procedures where efficacy is largely unproven? Journal of Medical Ethics 2018;44:27–31.

Johnson EK, Finlayson C, Rowell EE, Gosiengfiao Y, Pavone ME, Lockart B, Orwig KE, Brannigan RE, Woodruff TK. Fertility preservation for pediatric patients: current state and future possibilities. The Journal of urology. 2017 Jul 1;198(1):186–94.

Mattawanon N, Spencer JB, Schirmer DA, Tangpricha V. Fertility preservation options in transgender people: a review. Reviews in Endocrine and Metabolic Disorders. 2018 Sep;19:231–42.

Social Egg Freezing and Fertility Preservation

Katherine Cameron and Clarisa Gracia

Abstract This chapter summarizes ethical issues surrounding planned oocyte cryopreservation, or "oocyte cryopreservation to protect against a future threat of infertility." It proposes guidelines and suggestions for how clinicians involved in assisted reproduction can best counsel patients. It also highlights some of the larger societal implications and forces driving planned oocyte cryopreservation for both physician and patient to consider. We conclude that while it is ethical to offer planned oocyte cryopreservation, safeguards must be in place to ensure that this is done in the best interest of the patient and the technology is used responsibly. This includes recognizing at the time of a consult that patients may be feeling a sense of loss of control over their fertility and over their life goals, and discussion of family building options including the use of donor sperm for immediate conception should be included in the options presented to the patient. In addition, practitioners need to balance the natural desire to convey hope and respect for reproductive autonomy with the need to convey realistic treatment expectations. The informed consent process must emphasize that planned oocyte cryopreservation may not result in live birth, and the patient should understand the clinic's individual oocyte thaw success rates.

Keywords Cryopreservation · Egg freezing · Fertility preservation · Family building · Reproductive autonomy

K. Cameron (✉)
Division of Reproductive Endocrinology and Infertility, Johns Hopkins University School of Medicine, Baltimore, MD, USA

C. Gracia
Division of Reproductive Endocrinology and Infertility, University of Pennsylvania, Philadelphia, PA, USA

123

L. P. King, I. C. Band (eds.), *Case Studies in the Ethics of Assisted Reproduction*, https://doi.org/10.1007/978-3-031-41215-8_14

Case

A 30-year-old single woman who has never been pregnant expresses desire at a fertility clinic to freeze her eggs. Although she has never tried to get pregnant and has no reason to suspect infertility, she works at a technology company where social egg freezing has been a popular choice among young, career-driven women. She has been informed that stimulating a woman's ovaries and retrieving eggs is a two-week medical process that may present medical risks. The fertility specialist wants to ensure the patient is aware of the total cost including annual storage fees, all the medical risks associated with the procedure, and the fact that these eggs may likely never be needed.

Scope of the Question

This chapter will summarize and weigh ethical issues surrounding planned oocyte cryopreservation, or "oocyte cryopreservation to protect against a future threat of infertility." It will propose guidelines and suggestions on how clinicians involved in assisted reproduction might respond to a scenario similar to the one described above and can best counsel patients. It will also focus on some of the larger societal implications and forces driving planned oocyte cryopreservation for both physician and patient to consider. While oocyte cryopreservation in the face of an immediate gonadotoxic threat, such as chemotherapy or radiation, has been seen as ethically permissible since the lifting of the experimental label in 2012 [1], use of oocyte cryopreservation to protect against a future threat of infertility has only relatively recently been recognized as ethically permissible by the ASRM Ethics Committee [2]. This article will explore some of the developments leading to that advice, and the limitations and unknowns regarding the technology that are important for both clinician and patient to understand.

Background

The ability to cryopreserve reproductive tissues has allowed for significant advancements in reproductive medicine. After the first human birth from frozen sperm in 1953 [3], advancements in technology and freezing techniques ultimately allowed for the first human birth from a cryopreserved embryo in 1984 [4], followed by the first human birth from a frozen oocyte in 1986 [5].

More recently, the use of vitrification, which uses high initial concentrations of cryoprotectant and ultra-rapid cooling to solidify cells into a solid state without the formation of ice, has greatly improved the efficacy of oocyte cryopreservation. The challenges of cryopreservation unique to oocytes stem from the fragility of the metaphase-II egg related to its large size, high water content, and chromosomal rearrangement along the equatorial plate by a fragile meiotic spindle [6]. With the development of vitrification techniques that increase the success rates of the freeze-thaw process, oocyte cryopreservation had its experimental label lifted in 2012 [1], and an ASRM practice committee document deemed that oocyte cryopreservation was an acceptable technology for use to improve cumulative pregnancy rates in couples who are unable to cryopreserve embryos, and for patients who are facing infertility due to chemotherapy or other gonadotoxic therapies. At that point, several studies had demonstrated that using assisted reproductive technologies (ART) with frozen oocytes had success rates comparable to fresh oocytes [7–10], and newer evidence has continued to support that success rates of embryos from vitrified oocytes are similar to those of vitrified embryos [11, 12]. Notably, however, the 2012 practice committee document stated that, unlike oocyte cryopreservation for medical conditions, "there are not yet sufficient data to recommend oocyte cryo-preservation for the sole purpose of circumventing reproductive aging in healthy women because there are no data to support the safety, efficacy, ethics, emotional risks, and cost-effectiveness of oocyte cryopreservation for this indication."

Despite this caveat, oocyte cryopreservation has been used in practice with increasing frequency. According to data published in November 2017 from the Centers for Disease Control, in the year 2015 approximately 20% of all assisted reproductive technology (ART) cycles in the United States were for the sole purpose of banking oocytes [13]. A key tenet of protecting autonomy, discussed more below, is informed consent. It is critical that patients understand the limitations and unknowns of planned oocyte cryopreservation and the reality of success rates. As clinicians help guide patients through the decision to utilize planned oocyte cryo-preservation, it is important to consider the following.

First, most women are unaware of the magnitude of fertility decline that takes place as a result of advanced maternal age, which reduces both unassisted and assisted pregnancy rates after ART, most significantly after the age of 37 [14]. Many articles and videos in the lay media question these statistics but the evidence for fertility decline at these ages is robust. Multiple survey studies in both the UK and abroad have demonstrated significant 'knowledge gaps', or disconnects between reproductive plans and the reality of the risks of fertility decline. Both single and partnered women have repeatedly overestimated their own fertility potential and underestimated the risk of future childlessness despite planning to postpone preg-nancy [15–17]. These data suggest unrealistic expectations regarding the likelihood of unassisted conception with autologous oocytes at advanced ages in the surveyed populations.

Furthermore, the optimal timing of oocyte cryopreservation is also unknown. A 2015 study attempted to model the ideal timing of oocyte cryopreservation based on the SART registry data, and registries of marriage, pregnancy, and miscarriage rates [18]. That study found that the greatest improvement in the probability of achieving a live birth compared to no action occurred when oocyte cryopreservation was per-formed at age 37 (51.6% chance live birth compared to 21.9% with no action). However, the overall highest probability of live birth occurred with vitrification prior to age 34 (74%), though oocytes were much less likely to be ultimately utilized when cryopreserved earlier [18].

Finally, the steps of planned oocyte cryopreservation must be clearly explained to patients so that they can understand and weigh the medical risks. A 2017 survey demonstrated that while 87.2% of US women were aware of the option of oocyte cryopreservation, only 29.8% actually understood what the process entailed [19], which is approximately two weeks of gonadotropin injections and frequent ultrasound and lab monitoring, followed by transvaginal surgical procedure for oocyte extraction. Patients must also understand the risks and side effects of ovarian stimulation, the risks of egg retrieval, the costs of the procedure and storage, and the future need for intracytoplasmic sperm injection (ICSI) for future use.

Ethical Considerations

With this understanding of the nuances of planned oocyte cryopreservation, we can now turn our attention to examining the ethical considerations underpinning the technology. The first general question a practitioner should ask about a technology is, does it achieve 'good' overall, and how is that 'good' achieved? For instance, is there a medical good or social good associated with enacting the technology? In the case of medical technologies, this can specifically be achieved through the lens of ethical principlism, examining each of the principles (autonomy, beneficence, nonmaleficence, and justice) individually, with special weight given to autonomy, and then making a decision regarding the advisability of the technology overall.

Autonomy

In terms of autonomy, there is much that planned oocyte cryopreservation can offer, both to the individual, and theoretically to society. The raised awareness about the female reproductive window that arises from increased discourse promotes a better understanding of natural fertility and increases education for individuals and for the public at large.

The most touted ethical argument in favor of planned oocyte cryopreservation is that it allows for flexibility in life and career planning by promoting equal participation in the workforce during the most productive years, allowing women more time to choose a partner, and to become more financially stable if desired before embarking on a parenthood project [20].[1] In a 2018 survey examining attitudes of women who underwent cryopreservation of their oocytes, 88% reported a sense of increased

---

[1] Editor's note: In this chapter the author uses the terms female and woman as these terms are most typically used in the literature cited. However, it's important to recognize that fertility preservation is of concern to those who identify as female, male, or non-binary.

control over their reproductive planning, and 89% reported they were glad that they froze their eggs, even if they never returned to use them [21].

However, we must also consider if there are any harms to autonomy that befall women seeking this technology. Some have argued that encouraging planned oocyte cryopreservation, for a future vision of life that includes a future partner and perceived better job security, promotes societal prerequisites for parenting that are not fundamental to parenthood. In fact, empirical data suggests that the lack of a partner, more than other factors, encourages women to seek oocyte cryopreservation [22]. Counseling these women about donor sperm use for immediate parenthood may better fit their reproductive plans. Furthermore, for those women who might prefer to have children earlier in their lives, planned oocyte cryopreservation, particularly when advertised or paid for by an employer, may be seen as a way to encourage women to devote their most productive years to their job rather than to building a family. It may be argued that planned oocyte cryopreservation is applying a medical solution to a social issue that may be better served by instead things like advocating for universal childcare, flexible working hours, and more paid parental leave to allow single parenthood at a younger age to be more feasible for women [23].

There is also a potential argument to be made that planned oocyte cryopreservation may threaten a patient's autonomy by providing a false sense of security that does not actually exist. Increasingly, stories in the lay media regarding planned oocyte cryopreservation have featured tales of women who returned to use their cryopreserved oocytes only to have unsuccessful cycles, now at an age when they are too old to try again with autologous oocytes [24, 25]. This is particularly concerning when the patient received direct-to-consumer advertising involving 'fertility testing' and biased marketing that planned oocyte cryopreservation is an 'insurance policy'. Direct-to-consumer advertising in this space has been very aggressive, including tactics such as egg freezing 'parties' that encourage messages that imply a 'guarantee' [26, 27]. Patients must be adequately counseled that they may be basing large life decisions on a limited number of eggs, the success rate of each of which is only 3–7%, depending on the age at which vitrification occurs [28].

Non-maleficence

In terms of non-maleficence, the technologies and procedures associated with planned oocyte cryopreservation are the same as those used for infertile couples, and have proven safe and effective. While only short term, birth reports indicate no increase in congenital abnormalities in infants from cryopreserved oocytes compared with other IVF infants [29, 30]. However, data on the long term health outcomes in children born after oocyte cryopreservation are limited and there may be risks to offspring that are not yet known. For instance, recent studies have suggested that while the overall absolute risk is very low, there may be an increase in certain childhood cancers and imprinting disorders in offspring born as a result of ART [31–33]. It is also important to consider the potential risks associated with the procedure and the implications of the pregnancies that may result later in life. Pregnancies after the age of 40 are associated with greater risks of preeclampsia and pre-term delivery, and those over the age of 45 associated with higher odds of death, transfusion, cardiac arrest, and fetal demise [34].

Justice

In terms of justice, one must consider who is paying for these technologies, and whether the payer is approaching the relationship fairly. Does having an employer offer planned oocyte cryopreservation as a 'perk' of a job then entice women to delay having a family in order to focus on their employment? Who will pay storage fees in a situation where the cryopreservation was employer-funded, but the woman was later laid off or fired? For those without employer coverage, the costs of planned oocyte cryopreservation are often prohibitive, costing upwards of tens of thousands of dollars for the procedure and medications. In those cases, planned oocyte cryo-preservation is a technology only available to a privileged few, resulting in eco-nomic and likely ethnic/racial disparities [35].

Additional Considerations

Finally, an additional consideration involves the potential waste of resources (see "Disposition of Abandoned Cryopreserved Human Embryos" for a more extensive discussion on the topic). We know a large proportion of frozen oocytes will never be utilized [18], and current federal laws effectively prohibit those oocytes from being donated to any other parties for future use, even if that is what the patient ultimately desires when she determines that she herself does not wish to use her frozen eggs. Currently, if oocytes are to be eligible for donation to a third party who is a non-sexually intimate partner, a specific set of FDA-mandated testing is required to be performed prior to the time of cryopreservation, including a physical examination and screening for sexually-transmitted infections. This is a cumbersome process that is not routinely performed as the assumption is that the woman will return for her own oocytes. However, under current federal laws, it is not possible to donate previ-ously frozen oocytes without this testing if the woman does not use them herself.

Conclusion

On balance, it is likely ethical to offer planned oocyte cryopreservation, but safe-guards must be in place to ensure that this is done in the best interest of the patient and the technology is used responsibly. These include first recognizing at the time of a consult that women may be feeling a sense of loss of control over their fertility and over their life goals. Discussion of family building options including the use of donor sperm for immediate conception should be included in the options presented to the patient. In addition, practitioners need to balance the natural desire to convey hope and respect for reproductive autonomy with the need to convey realistic treatment expectations. The informed consent process must emphasize that planned oocyte cryopreservation may not result in a live birth, and the patient should understand the clinic's individual oocyte thaw success rates. There should also be a consideration for all patients undergoing planned oocyte cryopreservation to have a psychological consultation prior to undergoing the procedure.

As a final consideration, clinicians may have a responsibility to advocate for policies that will promote family building rather than fertility preservation as well as equitable access to this technology without ties to employment. There should be less aggressive direct-to-consumer advertising regarding oocyte cryopreservation, and more support of parental leave, flexible working hours, and increased childcare options.

Works Cited

1. Practice Committees of American Society for Reproductive Medicine, Society for Assisted Reproductive Technology. Mature oocyte cryopreservation: a guideline. Fertil Steril 2013;99:37–43.
2. Ethics Committee of the American Society for Reproductive Medicine Electronic address: asrm@asrm org, Ethics Committee of the American Society for Reproductive Medicine. Planned oocyte cryopreservation for women seeking to preserve future reproductive potential: an Ethics Committee opinion. Fertil Steril 2018;110:1022–8.
3. Sherman JK. Synopsis of the use of frozen human semen since 1964: state of the art of human semen banking. Fertil Steril 1973;24:397–412.
4. First baby born of frozen embryo. New York Times 1984:16.
5. Chen C. Pregnancy after human oocyte cryopreservation. Lancet 1986;1:884–6.
6. Baka SG, Toth TL, Veeck LL, Jones HW, Muasher SJ, Lanzendorf SE. Evaluation of the spindle apparatus of in-vitro matured human oocytes following cryopreservation. Hum Reprod 1995;10:1816–20.
7. Rienzi L, Romano S, Albricci L, Maggiulli R, Capalbo A, Baroni E, et al. Embryo development of fresh 'versus' vitrified metaphase II oocytes after ICSI: a prospective randomized sibling-oocyte study. Hum Reprod 2010;25:66–73.
8. Cobo A, Meseguer M, Remohi J, Pellicer A. Use of cryo-banked oocytes in an ovum donation programme: a prospective, randomized, controlled, clinical trial. Hum Reprod 2010;25:2239–46.
9. Parmegiani L, Cognigni GE, Bernardi S, Cuomo S, Ciampaglia W, Infante FE, et al. Efficiency of aseptic open vitrification and hermetical cryostorage of human oocytes. Reprod Biomed Online 2011;23:505–12.
10. Cobo A, Kuwayama M, Perez S, Ruiz A, Pellicer A, Remohi J. Comparison of concomitant outcome achieved with fresh and cryopreserved donor oocytes vitrified by the Cryotop method. Fertil Steril 2008;89:1657–64.

11. Doyle JO, Richter KS, Lim J, Stillman RJ, Graham JR, Tucker MJ. Successful elective and medically indicated oocyte vitrification and warming for autologous in vitro fertilization, with predicted birth probabilities for fertility preservation according to number of cryopreserved oocytes and age at retrieval. Fertil Steril 2016;105:459,66.e2.
12. Ho JR, Woo I, Louie K, Salem W, Jabara SI, Bendikson KA, *et al*. A comparison of live birth rates and perinatal outcomes between cryopreserved oocytes and cryopreserved embryos. J Assist Reprod Genet 2017;34:1359–66.
13. 2015 Assisted Reproductive Technology National Summary Report. Centers for Disease Control 2017.
14. Lyttle Schumacher B, Grover N, Mesen T, Steiner A, Mersereau J. Modeling of live-birth rates and cost-effectiveness of oocyte cryopreservation for cancer patients prior to high- and low-risk gonadotoxic chemotherapy. Hum Reprod 2017;32:2049–55.
15. Birch Petersen K, Hvidman HW, Sylvest R, Pinborg A, Larsen EC, Macklon KT, *et al*. Family intentions and personal considerations on postponing childbearing in childless cohabiting and single women aged 35-43 seeking fertility assessment and counselling. Hum Reprod 2015;30:2563–74.
16. Petersen KB. Individual fertility assessment and counselling in women of reproductive age. Dan Med J 2016;63:B5292.
17. Goldman KN, Grifo JA. Elective oocyte cryopreservation for deferred childbearing. Curr Opin Endocrinol Diabetes Obes 2016;23:458–64.
18. Mesen TB, Mersereau JE, Kane JB, Steiner AZ. Optimal timing for elective egg freezing. Fertil Steril 2015;103:1551–4.
19. Milman LW, Senapati S, Sammel MD, Cameron KD, Gracia C. Assessing reproductive choices of women and the likelihood of oocyte cryopreservation in the era of elective oocyte freezing. Fertil Steril 2017;107:1214,1222.e3.
20. Goold I, Savulescu J. In favour of freezing eggs for non-medical reasons. Bioethics 2009;23:47–58.
21. Greenwood EA, Pasch LA, Hastie J, Cedars MI, Huddleston HG. To freeze or not to freeze: decision regret and satisfaction following elective oocyte cryopreservation. Fertil Steril 2018;109:1097,1104.e1.
22. Reasons for egg freezing (oocyte cryopreservation) among U.S. women as of 2013. 2018.
23. Baldwin K, Culley L, Hudson N, Mitchell H. Reproductive technology and the life course: current debates and research in social egg freezing. Hum Fertil (Camb) 2014;17:170–9.
24. Ackerman R. Don't Put All Your (Frozen) Eggs in One Basket. New York Times 2019.
25. Richards SE. What Happened to All Those Frozen Eggs? New York Times 2019.
26. Ensor J. The Egg Whisperer- helping Silicon Valley women defy time. The Telegraph 2014.
27. McLaren L. How Women Are Freezing The Biological Clock. Newsweek 2014.
28. Goldman RH, Racowsky C, Farland LV, Munne S, Ribustello L, Fox JH. Predicting the likelihood of live birth for elective oocyte cryopreservation: a counseling tool for physicians and patients. Hum Reprod 2017;32:853–9.
29. Noyes N, Porcu E, Borini A. Over 900 oocyte cryopreservation babies born with no apparent increase in congenital anomalies. Reprod Biomed Online 2009;18:769–76.
30. Levi-Setti PE, Borini A, Patrizio P, Bolli S, Vigiliano V, De Luca R, *et al*. ART results with frozen oocytes: data from the Italian ART registry (2005-2013). J Assist Reprod Genet 2016;33:123–8.
31. Hargreave M, Jensen A, Hansen MK, Dehlendorff C, Winther JF, Schmiegelow K, *et al*. Association Between Fertility Treatment and Cancer Risk in Children. JAMA 2019;322:2203–10.
32. Spector LG, Brown MB, Wantman E, Letterie GS, Toner JP, Doody K, *et al*. Association of In Vitro Fertilization With Childhood Cancer in the United States. JAMA Pediatr 2019;173:e190392.

33. Lazaraviciute G, Kauser M, Bhattacharya S, Haggarty P, Bhattacharya S. A systematic review and meta-analysis of DNA methylation levels and imprinting disorders in children conceived by IVF/ICSI compared with children conceived spontaneously. Hum Reprod Update 2015;21:555–7.
34. Grotegut CA, Chisholm CA, Johnson LN, Brown HL, Heine RP, James AH. Medical and obstetric complications among pregnant women aged 45 and older. PLoS One 2014;9:e96237.
35. Petropanagos A, Cattapan A, Baylis F, Leader A. Social egg freezing: risk, benefits and other considerations. CMAJ 2015;187:666–9.

Disposition of Abandoned Cryopreserved Human Embryos

Saioa Torrealday, Sangita K. Jindal, and Lubna Pal

Abstract IVF cycles often produce supernumerary cryopreserved embryos, which may be unused when a patient or couple decides against pursuing additional fertility attempts. In cases where the patient or couple has not provided instructions regarding embryo disposition and is unreachable after reasonable efforts by the clinic, the embryos are considered "abandoned." This chapter focuses on the ethical issues that ART clinics face related to the disposition of abandoned cryopreserved embryos that are kept in storage. Key ethical principles include: (1) autonomy of the individual(s) who provided the gametes to determine the fate of the embryos, (2) justice and the high cost of embryo storage fees which impact dispositional decisions, (3) the obligation to respect the conceptualization of embryos by an individual or couple when discussing the disposal of embryos and (4) the need for caution against the assumption that all abandoned embryos are undesired. To avoid situations where embryos are abandoned, clinics should require that patients specify their preferences for future embryo disposition, including in the case of loss of contact between patients and the clinic.

Keywords Abandoned embryo · Disposed embryo · Supernumerary embryo · Embryo freezing · Embryo storage

S. Torrealday (✉)
Department of Gynecologic Surgery and Obstetrics, Walter Reed National Military Medical Center, Bethesda, MD, USA

S. K. Jindal
Department of Obstetrics, Gynecology and Women's Health, Albert Einstein College of Medicine, Bronx, NY, USA

Montefiore's Institute for Reproductive Medicine and Health, Hartsdale, NY, USA

L. Pal
Division of Reproductive Endocrinology & Infertility, Department of Obstetrics, Gynecology & Reproductive Sciences, Yale School of Medicine, New Haven, CT, USA

L. P. King, I. C. Band (eds.), *Case Studies in the Ethics of Assisted Reproduction*, https://doi.org/10.1007/978-3-031-41215-8_15

Case

A 37-year-old G2P2002 woman with proven tubal disease underwent an in vitro fertilization (IVF) cycle. She had three good quality blastocysts available on the day of transfer, and subsequently underwent a single embryo transfer. The patient and her husband were counseled on the various disposition options for the remaining two embryos. The couple elected to cryopreserve the two embryos in efforts to preserve options should the cycle be unsuccessful or possibly expand their family in the future if she successfully became pregnant (see chapter "Social Egg Freezing and Fertility Preservation" for additional discussion of fertility preservation). The embryos were onsite at the Assisted Reproductive Technology (ART) clinic and the couple paid the annual storage fee. The couple successfully conceived a healthy female infant from the IVF cycle.

Five years have passed, and the ART clinic has not been able to contact the couple regarding the disposition of the embryos. There was no written documentation regarding the couple's long-term desires on file. The couple has not paid embryo storage fees for the past three years despite numerous attempts to contact them. Certified letters have been sent in efforts to reach the couple, all of which have been returned unacknowledged. The gamete/embryo storage capacity of the ART clinic is starting to reach a critical limit and repeated efforts are being made by the clinic staff to contact the patient/couple to obtain disposition instructions for the abandoned embryos.

Scope of the Question

This chapter will focus on the ethical issues that ART clinics face related to the disposition of abandoned cryopreserved embryos that are kept in storage and therefore regarded as a responsibility of the facility. For patients who have decided against pursuing additional fertility attempts with their remaining embryo/s that are in storage, the most chosen options for eventual disposition are: thawing and discarding the embryo/s, donation of embryo/s for use by other infertile couples, and donation for use in research. The less utilized option is where the female partner chooses to undergo the transfer of the frozen thawed embryo such that there is negligible to no chance of the embryo transfer resulting in a conception. Transfer of thawed embryo at a time in the menstrual cycle that is well outside the implantation window or transferring the embryo in the vagina rather than into the uterus are two accepted methods [1]. An option that is often overlooked is that of *inaction*, or simply leaving the embryo/s cryopreserved indefinitely with no specified plan.

Unfortunately, there are cases in which the individual patient or couple has not provided explicit instructions regarding embryo disposition and are unreachable. When individuals or couples who can make the disposition decision cannot be reached despite numerous attempts to contact them, the embryos are considered "abandoned." [2] [1] To avoid this situation, many clinics now require that patients specify their preferences for future embryo disposition, including in the case of loss of contact between patients and the clinic, to reduce future challenges of abandoned cryopreserved embryos. This requirement should be widely implemented.

Background

The 2016 ART National Summary Report notes frozen embryo transfers (FET) from non-donor oocytes accounted for 32.7% (86,266 cycles) of all ART cycles (263,577 cycles) performed that year [5]. The percentage of transfers resulting in live births was higher for cryopreserved embryos using nondonor oocytes than with transfer of fresh embryos (45.9% vs. 36.3%) in 2016 [5]. The increasing success of FET cycles can be attributed to switching from slow cooling to rapid cooling protocols, commonly known as embryo vitrification, in conjunction with optimization of the uterine milieu during FET cycles. These successes have caused shifts in clinical management such that increasingly fertility clinics are recommending to "cryopreserve all" embryos resulting from IVF cycles followed by transfer of a thawed embryo in a future FET cycle. With this change in paradigm, embryo cryopreservation has become common practice.

Current IVF cycles frequently produce supernumerary embryos. It is the responsibility of individual clinics to ensure that they have documented contact information for the responsible individual/s and have explicit consent from the patient and partner (if applicable) regarding the disposition and dispositional decisional control of any stored embryo/s. Despite this guidance, it is estimated that abandoned embryos comprise anywhere from 1% to as high as 5–7% of the embryos stored in a facility [6, 7].

Managing cryopreserved reproductive tissues in an IVF laboratory requires skilled personnel and specialized equipment. Accredited IVF labs are required to meet minimum standards and requirements including, but not limited to, checking tanks several times per week or continuous monitoring via a probe, continuous alarms that are tested at least quarterly, and enough liquid nitrogen supply for emergencies [8]. Cryo storage tanks may need to be replaced or supplemented as they age or as the number of cryopreserved embryos accumulates, adding to the already significant expenses incurred by the IVF lab [9].

Although there is some legal uncertainty surrounding the issues of embryo abandonment, ASRM has suggested it is ethically acceptable for the facility to consider the embryos abandoned and dispose if at least 5 years have passed since contact with an individual or couple, diligent efforts have been made to contact the person,

---

[1] Editors' note. In some countries "freezing" embryos is not permitted and in some with highly restrictive abortion legislation, including some states in America, disposition of embryos without intended pregnancy violates legal restrictions and is not possible. These situations are not covered in this chapter.

and no written documentation exists concerning disposition [2]. The ASRM opinion stresses that the abandoned embryos must never be donated to another couple or used for research or investigational purposes [2, 10].

Ethical Considerations

Infertility specialists, IVF laboratory directors, clinical embryologists and ART facilities face several ethical dilemmas with respect to the handling and disposal of abandoned embryos. The key ethical principles of autonomy, justice, non-maleficence, and beneficence must be considered when addressing the topic of embryo disposal, particularly given the sensitive nature of reproductive medicine.

Autonomy

Patients whose gametes have contributed to the creation of the embryos must hold the right to determine the fate of their embryos. After adequate counseling, the disposition desires of the individual, or couple, must be appropriately respected by the ART clinic. Furthermore, the individual/s should be given complete freedom to change their disposition plans, should their circumstances or their preferences change. Since there are typically two individuals involved in the creation of an embryo, both parties must agree upon the disposition, unless legal authority has granted decision-making power to one of the two, or rarely to a third person.

The ASRM opinion previously gives guidance and suggests a 5-year time limit in the setting of abandonment after which it may be ethically reasonable to discard embryos. However, ASRM also states that there is no legal precedent regarding specified time limit and this guidance should be used with some caution. Without firm legal protections, health care professionals may err on the side of caution by keeping the embryos frozen for perpetuity, a costly endeavor that in turn might affect a clinic's ability to provide care to others. Many IVF programs are resistant to discarding abandoned embryos [12].

Justice

IVF treatment cycles are costly; the expense can escalate into thousands of dollars to cover the cost of the medications, monitoring, oocyte retrieval, IVF laboratory fees for the creation and culture of the embryo/s and the eventual embryo transfer. Although there are some states that now mandate insurance coverage for infertility treatments, such as IVF, this is not universally offered across the United States. For some individuals the additional costs of cryopreservation of the embryos, and the annual fees to cover the cost of storage of unused embryos are additional financial burdens that cannot be undertaken or sustained. A study that examined the effects on the implementation of newly levied embryo storage fee on embryo disposal activity in a clinic that previously offered free embryo storage demonstrated that the number of disposal requests increased from 0% to 5% to nearly 18% upon institution of the monthly fee. This study highlighted that financial considerations are relevant to dispositional decisions [13]. The significant financial burden of ART is reflected in the socioeconomic and racial disparities that are evident in regards to access to ART services. The additive cost of embryo cryopreservation is likely to widen this socio-economic divide such that individuals of lesser financial means are rendered less likely to elect to cryopreserve excess embryos.

There is no legal guidance in the United States regarding the appropriate period of time ahead of discarding abandoned embryos. Several other countries have addressed this issue head on with legislation. Some allow 5 years of embryo storage (Denmark), whereas others allow a 10-year limit (UK, New Zealand) [14–16]. In some jurisdictions, the regulation time period is fixed whereas in others, extensions are allowed if requested by the patient [12]. Time constraints can facilitate decision-making regarding embryo status and thus help address the issue of abandoned embryos; yet, they can negatively impact individual patients with unique constraints and needs that may wish to postpone childbearing until after the designated time frame. For those patients, moving embryos off-site to a long-term storage facility with an annual storage fee may be a reasonable option, yet this option does not address disparities in access based on funds.

Non-maleficence

One of the challenges of discussing embryo disposal with patients is ensuring respect for the conceptualization of embryos by the individual or couple. For some patients, an embryo is a collection of cells, whereas for others, an embryo may be considered an unborn child [17–19]. Caution must be used and sensitivity is advised when counseling patients regarding the embryo disposition decision, particularly when disposal by discarding or use for research purposes are discussed. By strictly following an individual or couple's guidance regarding disposition, harm can be avoided.

Beneficence

Embryo cryopreservation has allowed many families the ability to postpone childbearing for medical or social indications, while still allowing them the ability to achieve their desired family size. Yet, the promise of this technology comes with the added burden of determining disposition of unused embryos.

Approximately 70% of interviewed patients revealed distress upon facing a disposition related decision [20]. This indecisiveness may explain the lack of response or inaction, which can lead to extended storage of embryos or even abandonment [12, 21]. Caution is merited against an assumption that all abandoned embryos may be undesired. Clinics should have some flexibility on how they treat stored embryos for which payments are delayed or when there is minimal ongoing contact with the patients.

Conclusion

The increasing application and advances in embryo cryopreservation options has transformed the field of ART, and the utilization of cryopreserved embryos in FET cycles has become a mainstay in infertility management. More facilities are now including specific questions regarding the desired disposition of embryos in the case of lost contact, lack of payment, or unforeseen situations such as divorce or death. Documenting patient preferences for embryo disposition around the time that they begin cryopreserving embryos is best practice to avoid challenges associated with abandoned embryos. Unfortunately, these new implementation strategies and processes will not address those abandoned embryos which exist in storage and predate any changes in documentation.

Works Cited

1. Ethics Committee of the American Society of Reproductive Medicine. Compassionate transfer: patient requests for embryo transfer for nonreproductive purposes. Fertil Steril 2020; 113(1):62–65.
2. Ethics Committee of the American Society of Reproductive Medicine. Disposition of abandoned embryos: a committee opinion. Fertil Steril 2013; 99(7):1848–1849.
3. Trounson A, Mohr L. Human pregnancy following cryopreservation, thawing and transfer of an eight-cell embryo. Nature 1983; 305:707–709.
4. Chen C. Pregnancy after human oocyte cryopreservation. Lancet 1986; 1(8486):884–886.
5. 2016 Assisted Reproductive Technology (ART) Report: 2016 Assisted Reproductive Technology National Summary Report. Available at: https://www.cdc.gov/art/reports/2016/national-summary.html
6. Walsh APH, Tsar OM, Baldwin PM, Shkrobot LV, Sills ES. Who abandons embryos after IVF? Ir Med J 2010 103(4):107–110.
7. Hoffman DI, Zellman GL, Fair CC, Mayer JF, Zeitz JG, Gibbons WE, et al. Cryopreserved embryos in the United States and their availability for research. Fertil Steril 2003; 79(5):1063–1069.
8. 2019 College of American Pathologists Accreditation Checklist, College of American Pathologists, Sept 17, 2019.
9. Practice Committee of The American Society for Reproductive medicine. Cryo storage of reproductive tissues in the IVF laboratory: a committee opinion. Fertil Steril, in press.

10. Ethics Committee of the American Society of Reproductive Medicine. Ethics in embryo research: a position statement by the ASRM Ethics in Embryo Research Task Force and ASRM Ethics Committee. Fertil Steril 2020; 113(2): 270–294.
11. Greco E, Minasi MG, Fiorentino F. Healthy babies after intrauterine transfer of mosaic aneuploid blastocysts. NEJM 2015; 373(21):2089–2090.
12. Cattapan A, Baylis F. Frozen in perpetuity: 'abandoned embryos' in Canada. Reprod Biomed Soc Online 2016; 1(2):104–112.
13. Brzyski RG, Binkley PA, Pierce D, Eddy CA. Impact of implementation of an embryo storage fee on embryo disposal activity. Fertil Steril 2000; 74(4): 813–815.
14. Denmark, 1997. Lov om kunstig befrugtnig i forbindelse med laegelig behandling, diagnostik og forskning m.v (Law on artificial fertilization in connection with medical treatment, diagnosis and research, etc.) p. 460.
15. New Zealand, 2010. Human Assisted Reproductive Technology (Storage) Amendment Act 2010 10/117.
16. United Kingdom. Department of Health, 2009. Explanatory Memorandum to the Human Fertilisation and Embryology Authority (Statutory storage period for embryos and gametes) (Amendment regulations) No. 2581.
17. Klock SC. Embryo disposition: the forgotten "child" of in vitro fertilization. Int J Feril Womens Med. 2004; 49(1):19–23.
18. Nachtigall RD, Becker G, Friese C, Butler A, MacDougall K. Parents' conceptualization of their frozen embryos complicates the disposition decision. Fertil Steril 2005; 84(2):431–434.
19. Simopoulou M, Sfakianoudis K, Giannelou P, Rapani A, Maziotis E, Tsiolou P, et al. Discarding IVF embryos: reporting on global practices. J Assis Reprod Gen 2019; 36: 2447–2457.
20. Bruno C, Dudkiewicz-Sibony C, Berthaut I, Weil E, Brunet L, Fortier C, et al. Survey of 243 ART patients having made a final disposition about their surplus cryopreserved embryos: the crucial role of symbolic embryo representation. Hum Reprod 2016; 31(7):1508–1514.
21. Svanberg AS, Boivin J, Bergh T. Factors influencing the decision to use or discard cryopreserved embryos. Acta Obstet Gynecol Scand 2001; 80(9):849–855.

Access to Care for the Underserved

Isabelle C. Band and Louise P. King

Abstract In the United States, unmet needs for infertility treatment are high, and the proportion of patients that are "underserved" exceeds that in most other fields (ASRM Ethics Committee, https://www.asrm.org/about-us/initiatives/diversity-task-force/dei/asrm-task-force-on-diversity-equity-and-inclusion-issues-statement-recommendations/, 2021). Infertility may be detrimental to an individual or family's health, social status, family stability and psychological wellness (ASRM Ethics Committee, https://www.asrm.org/about-us/initiatives/diversity-task-force/dei/asrm-task-force-on-diversity-equity-and-inclusion-issues-statement-recommendations/, 2021). This chapter explores the disparities that prevent equitable access to treatment and impact treatment outcomes in the U.S. The most salient barrier to treatment access is financial; many patients lack access due to its high cost and limited coverage by insurance. Only a portion of U.S. states mandate coverage of infertility testing and treatment, and several state mandates carry significant restrictions (RESOLVE, https://resolve.org/learn/financial-resources-for-family-building/insurance-coverage/insurance-coverage-by-state/, 2021). In addition to financial barriers, this chapter explores ethnic, racial, and geographic barriers to care. Reproductive justice demands that persons have equitable opportunities to have children when they wish to and are free from serious medical contraindications (SisterSong, https://www.sistersong.net/reproductive-justice, 2022). Physicians have an ethical obligation to engage with payors, employers, and policymakers to advocate for equitable and affordable care. In addition, REI clinics should recruit a diverse and informed workforce, require cultural competence trainings, identify cost-effective infertility treatments and research how to improve treatment

I. C. Band (✉)
Icahn School of Medicine at Mount Sinai, New York, NY, USA

L. P. King
Center for Bioethics, Harvard Medical School, Boston, MA, USA

© The Author(s), under exclusive license to Springer Nature Switzerland AG 2023
L. P. King, I. C. Band (eds.), *Case Studies in the Ethics of Assisted Reproduction*, https://doi.org/10.1007/978-3-031-41215-8_16

141

outcomes across diverse populations (ASRM Ethics Committee, https://www.asrm. org/about-us/initiatives/diversity-task-force/dei/asrm-task-force-on-diversity-equity-and-inclusion-issues-statement-recommendations/, 2021).

Keywords Underserved · Disparities · Mandated insurance coverage · Reproductive justice · Equity

Case

C.A. is a 25-year-old woman who presents for infertility after attempts at pregnancy with her partner for over one year. She has a remote history of chlamydia treated with antibiotics when symptomatic with cervicitis at age 18. Imaging studies (hysterosalpingogram) reveal possible tubal disease. C.A. lives in a state with mandated health insurance coverage for infertility services but she has "safety net" insurance not subject to the mandate. If she wishes to proceed with assisted reproduction she must pay tens of thousands of dollars out of pocket. She can't afford this. She notes that when younger she had no access to sex education or preventative health services. She did not understand that she could protect herself from sexually transmitted diseases with condom use nor that these diseases could affect her fertility.

Scope of the Question

This chapter will explore economic, racial, ethnic and geographic disparities that prevent equitable access to fertility treatment and impact treatment outcomes in the United States. We will then explore the ethical considerations at play in the case outlined above.

Background

Involuntary childlessness due to infertility can have a profound negative impact on individuals, causing medical, social, economic and psychological harm. Approximately 7.4 million women in the U.S. or 12.1% of women of reproductive age face challenges in having children due to impaired fecundity [1]. About 9.4% of men are subfertile or nonsurgically sterile [2].

During World War II, the U.S. Supreme Court defined procreation as "one of the basic civil rights of man… fundamental to the very existence and survival of the race [3]." The right to reproductive liberty can be understood as the right to make reproductive decisions free from government interference [4]. The Inter-American Court of Human Rights reaffirmed that right when it overturned Costa Rica's 12-year ban on IVF [4]. Although there has been some debate on whether infertility constitutes a disease that merits "medically necessary" treatment, the World Health Organization stated that "infertility generates disability (an impairment of function), and thus access to health care falls under the Convention on the Rights of Persons with Disability [5]." Reproductive justice is defined as "the human right to maintain personal bodily autonomy, have children, not have children, and parent the children we have in safe and sustainable communities [6]." In spite of reproduction being recognized as a basic human right, "economic, racial, ethnic, geographic, and other disparities exist in access to fertility treatments and in treatment outcomes [5]."

Unmet need for infertility treatment is high in the United States, and the proportion of patients that can be considered "underserved" exceeds that in most other fields. In 2009, an expert panel estimated that only 24% of the need for infertility treatment was being met in the US [4]. An analysis of the 2015–2017 National Survey of Family Growth found that only 10% of women aged 18–49 report that they or their partner have ever discussed with a doctor ways to help them become pregnant [7]. In 2017, approximately 1.7% of children born in the US were conceived using ART, with the proportions highest in the Northeast [8]. Rates of children conceived via ART are higher in Europe overall and especially in countries where IVF is publicly funded (e.g., Denmark, Sweden) [4].

Infertility may be detrimental to an individual or family's overall health, social status and family stability. Infertility can also contribute to psychological disorders such as depression. Though improving access is critical, research suggests that current infertility treatments are not successful for all patients [4]. Biological causes of infertility (e.g., fibroids, PCOS) may vary by race, ethnicity and sex. Studies have also found that minority women typically seek treatment after a longer duration of infertility which may contribute to lower pregnancy rates [4].When financial barriers are removed, use of assisted reproductive services among Black women increases [9]. However, even in the absence of financial barriers, Black, Asian, Latina and Native American women undergoing fertility treatment experience lower pregnancy and live birth rates compared to Caucasian women [10–12]. Women of color using egg donors also experience worse outcomes compared to Caucasian women [13]. Additional research along different demographic lines is needed to optimize treatment.

Financial, Economic and Insurance Barriers

One of the most salient barriers to infertility treatment access is a financial one. Many patients in the United States lack access to infertility treatment due to its high cost and limited coverage by private insurance and Medicaid. The cost of one cycle of IVF including medications was about $25,000 in 2020 and is likely higher today due to the rising cost of healthcare – a cost that exceeds 50% of the average American's annual disposable income [14]. It is also important to note that many patients require multiple cycles of IVF before achieving pregnancy, making treatment increasingly unaffordable. In addition to costs of treatment and medications, there are also high costs associated with diagnostics, genetic testing, donor gamete use and storage. Even non-IVF fertility treatments can be cost-prohibitive for individuals of median income level or below. As a result, persons of lower to average socioeconomic status are underrepresented in the population of fertility clinic patients [4].

In the United States, insurance coverage of infertility treatment varies by the patient's state of residence and the size of the patient's employer, for those with employer-sponsored insurance. While certain fertility services, such as diagnostic testing, are covered by most insurance providers, many more expensive fertility treatments (e.g., IVF, IUI) are not considered "medically necessary" and therefore are not covered [7]. As of June 2022, 20 U.S. states have passed fertility insurance coverage laws. Fourteen of those laws cover IVF, and 12 have fertility preservation laws for medically-induced infertility [15]. US states have laws in effect requiring certain plans to cover at least some infertility treatments ("mandate to cover"). However, these mandates do not apply to health plans that are funded directly by employers (self-funded). Employee Retirement Income Act (ERISA) holds that state mandates do not apply to plans that are self-insured and thus curtails the benefit of mandated coverage [7].

Among states with mandates, nine states (CT, DE, IL, MD, MA, NJ, NH, NY, RI) have a benchmark plan that includes coverage for some infertility services for most individual and small group plans in that state [4]. California and Texas have a "mandate to offer", meaning that group plans must offer at least one policy with infertility coverage, but employers are not required to choose those plans [7]. Only one state – New York – has a Medicaid program that covers infertility treatment, but no Medicaid program covers intrauterine insemination or in-vitro fertilization, further widening the gap for low-income people, even if they have insurance coverage [7].

Though mandated insurance coverage may result in better access to care, several state mandates carry restrictions (e.g., mandates only apply to certain insurers or have monetary caps). For example, the Arkansas mandate specifies that only married persons can qualify for insurance coverage for infertility treatment; the mandate specifies that a patient's eggs be fertilized with her spouse's sperm [15].

LGBTQ individuals face heightened barriers to accessing treatment because they often do not meet definitions of "infertility" that would qualify them for covered services. The World Health Organization (WHO) describes infertility as "disease of the male or female reproductive system defined by the failure to achieve a pregnancy after 12 months or more of regular unprotected sexual intercourse [16]." This definition notably excludes same-sex couples or asexual persons. Insurance policies that use the WHO's definition of infertility likely preclude these persons from gaining access to family building technologies such as donor sperm, IUI and gestational surrogates. Transgender individuals undergoing gender-affirming care may not meet criteria for "iatrogenic infertility" that would qualify them for fertility preservation coverage [7].

State-mandated insurance has increased per-capita usage of infertility treatments threefold [4]. In addition, mandated insurance coverage has been linked to better public health outcomes, including a lower rate of high-order multiple births and twin births [4]. Researchers believe that better insurance coverage of infertility treatments has reduced financial pressures to transfer more than one to two embryos in a single cycle. A lower rate of multiple births yields better maternal and newborn health. Broader insurance coverage is critical because it gives more patients access to infertility treatment without requiring that they take on significant financial burden or hardship [4]. It also allows physicians to deliver evidence-based, medically indicated care that is not contingent on what a patient can afford and spares physicians from turning patients away due to their inability to pay.

While insurance mandates are important, they only benefit individuals with private insurance and thus their benefits do not extend to the uninsured, or to those who receive coverage through Medicaid or from employers who are self-insured or too small to be subjected to the mandate. The Affordable Care Act of 2010 presented an opportunity to expand infertility treatment coverage however there is little evidence that it achieved that result [4].

Other Disparities in Access

In addition to financial and insurance-related barriers, ethnic and racial barriers to care persist in the United States. According to the most recent National Survey of Family Growth (1982–2010), black women have a higher rate of infertility compared to white women [17]. However, infertility treatment is utilized disproportionately by non-Hispanic Caucasian women; non-Hispanic Caucasian women (15%) are about twice as likely as Hispanic (7.5%) and non-Hispanic black women (8.0%) to have used medical help to achieve pregnancy [17]. Asian women are also twice as likely to wait at least 2 years to present for infertility treatment compared to Caucasian women (43.9% vs. 24.6%) [18].

Cultural beliefs and family values may contribute to these disparities in access to care [18]. Among black, Hispanic, Muslim and Asian populations in the US, communication differences, cultural stigmas against infertility and infertility treatment, cultural emphasis on privacy or bad previous experiences with the US healthcare system may dissuade members of groups from seeking infertility treatment. Where relevant, language barriers may also play a role in low utilization of infertility treatments by non-English speaking minority groups [18].

Some health care professionals may have conscious or unconscious biases about who deserves to be a parent and to receive treatment – these biases may impact patient experiences with doctors and may dissuade people of color, single people and same sex couples from seeking out treatment [19]. Women of color, specifically, have reported that some physicians ignore their concerns in interactions [4]. Some physicians refuse to treat unpartnered or same sex couples, though the ASRM clearly states this is not acceptable. LGBTQI+ individuals and couples face a number of legal and medical barriers to becoming parents and often struggle to be recognized as intended parents. In addition, infertility treatment is time intensive and typically requires time away from work and the ability to travel to medical facilities that may be geographically distant. This is not feasible for all prospective patients [19].

Ethical Considerations

Reproductive justice demands that persons have equitable opportunities to have children when they wish to do so, taking into account any medical contraindications or risk of serious harm [6]. This concept incorporates respect for a person's autonomous decision making. As described in this chapter, there are access disparities in the United States and elsewhere that severely compromise the ability of many classes of people to access assisted reproduction. While this problem is pervasive and affects 100,000 s of people in our country, it receives little attention.

Recommendations

Because reproduction is a fundamental interest and human right, access and outcome disparities warrant correction. The fact that infertility treatment is accessible primarily to non-Hispanic Caucasians of average or above average income perpetuates the idea that infertility treatment is a luxury or lifestyle choice rather than treatment of a disease or a goal of medical care to ensure both mental and physical health [4].

Lack of universal insurance coverage or access discriminates against significant groups of people and inhibits them from obtaining medical assistance to reproduce. Though adoption is a suitable family-building path for some [1], it would be non-sustainable and discriminatory to suggest that it be the sole means for those struggling with infertility [4]. Cost should not be a barrier to improving access to infertility treatment because the cost of insurance coverage of infertility treatment relative to other insurance costs is modest. In a 2006 survey, 91% of employers that offered an infertility benefit reported that infertility treatment did not add significant cost. In addition, Massachusetts, which instituted the most comprehensive infertility insurance mandate in the US with no monetary cap, reports only modest costs for coverage [4].

Improved access to ART serves an ethical good and social justice end. The ASRM's 2020–2025 Strategic Plan listed as a goal to "expand access to reproductive care by addressing social, cultural, demographic, and economic barriers [20]." The organization noted that one of its strategies for achieving that goal is to "engage with other medical and scientific organizations, payors, employers, and policymakers in advocating for equitable, inclusive, and affordable access to reproductive health and reproductive care [20]." The ASRM also established a task force on diversity, equity and inclusion (DEI Task Force), which has made a number of recommendations on how to reduce and eventually eliminate disparities in health access and outcomes [19]. We acknowledge that significantly improving access to quality treatment for all patients will require significant research, work and education. We recommend the following initiatives, to help combat existing barriers:

- Expand the recruitment and retention of a diverse, informed workforce and recruit multilingual staff and physicians [19]
- Establish practices in underserved geographic areas [4]
- Aim to hold hours outside of Monday through Friday, 9 AM-5 PM, and offer telemedicine visits in order to improve access for those who work full time or who are geographically located farther away from infertility clinics [18]
- Require cultural competence training to ensure physicians avoid selecting treatments based solely on their own religious beliefs or unconscious/conscious biases [4]
- Identify and evaluate more cost-effective infertility treatments, even if their success rate is lower (e.g., minimal-stimulation protocols, lab techniques that use fewer resources, natural cycle IVF, in vitro maturation, vaginal incubation) [18]
- Educate health insurance companies and self-insured employers about best practices in infertility treatment given that many are not aware of technologies that can reduce iatrogenic multiple pregnancy
- Promote inclusive definitions (i.e., to extend access to the "socially infertile") and reduce infertility-related stigma in diverse populations through education about signs and treatments of infertility [19]
- Advocate for universal, inclusive insurance coverage of high-quality infertility treatment for all patients, regardless of their race, ethnicity, state of residence, insurance type, sexual orientation or marital status [4]
- Research how to improve infertility treatment outcomes across diverse populations [4]

Works Cited

1. NSFG – Listing I – Key Statistics from the National Survey of Family Growth. Published November 6, 2019. Accessed July 11, 2022. https://www.cdc.gov/nchs/nsfg/key_statistics/i.htm
2. Chandra A, Stephen EH. Infertility and Impaired Fecundity in the United States, 1982–2010: Data From the National Survey of Family Growth. 2013;(67):19.
3. Skinner v. Oklahoma ex rel. Williamson, 316 U.S. 535 (1942). Justia Law. Accessed April 13, 2023. https://supreme.justia.com/cases/federal/us/316/535/
4. Ethics Committee of the American Society for Reproductive Medicine. Disparities in access to effective treatment for infertility in the United States: an Ethics Committee opinion. Fertility and Sterility Dialog. Published February 11, 2021. Accessed July 11, 2022. http://www.fert-stertdialog.com/posts/32465
5. Ethics Committee of the American Society for Reproductive Medicine. Disparities in access to effective treatment for infertility in the United States: an Ethics Committee opinion. *Fertil Steril*. 2015;104(5):1104–1110. https://doi.org/10.1016/j.fertnstert.2015.07.1139

6. Reproductive Justice. Sister Song. Accessed July 14, 2022. https://www.sistersong.net/reproductive-justice

7. Weigel G, Ranji U, Long M, 2020. Coverage and Use of Fertility Services in the U.S. KFF. Published September 15, 2020. Accessed July 12, 2022. https://www.kff.org/womens-health-policy/issue-brief/coverage-and-use-of-fertility-services-in-the-u-s/

8. State-Specific Assisted Reproductive Technology Surveillance | CDC. Published December 23, 2021. Accessed July 12, 2022. https://www.cdc.gov/art/state-specific-surveillance/index.html

9. Feinberg EC, Larsen FW, Catherino WH, Zhang J, Armstrong AY. Comparison of assisted reproductive technology utilization and outcomes between Caucasian and African American patients in an equal-access-to-care setting. *Fertil Steril*. 2006;85(4):888–894. https://doi.org/10.1016/j.fertnstert.2005.10.028

10. McQueen DB, Schufreider A, Lee SM, Feinberg EC, Uhler ML. Racial disparities in in vitro fertilization outcomes. *Fertil Steril*. 2015;104(2):398–402.e1. https://doi.org/10.1016/j.fertnstert.2015.05.012

11. Humphries LA, Chang O, Humm K, Sakkas D, Hacker MR. Influence of race and ethnicity on in vitro fertilization outcomes: systematic review. *Am J Obstet Gynecol*. 2016;214(2):212.e1–212.e17. https://doi.org/10.1016/j.ajog.2015.09.002

12. Craig LB, Weedin EA, Walker WD, Janitz AE, Hansen KR, Peck JD. Racial and Ethnic Differences in Pregnancy Rates Following Intrauterine Insemination with a Focus on American Indians. *J Racial Ethn Health Disparities*. 2018;5(5):1077–1083. https://doi.org/10.1007/s40615-017-0456-8

13. Zhou X, McQueen DB, Schufreider A, Lee SM, Uhler ML, Feinberg EC. Black recipients of oocyte donation experience lower live birth rates compared with White recipients. *Reprod Biomed Online*. 2020;40(5):668–673. https://doi.org/10.1016/j.rbmo.2020.01.008

14. Klein A. I.V.F. is Expensive. Here's How to Bring Down the Cost. *The New York Times*. https://www.nytimes.com/article/ivf-treatment-costs-guide.html. Published April 18, 2020. Accessed April 13, 2023.

15. Insurance Coverage by State | RESOLVE: The National Infertility Association. Published August 27, 2021. Accessed July 12, 2022. https://resolve.org/learn/financial-resources-for-family-building/insurance-coverage/insurance-coverage-by-state/

16. Infertility. Accessed April 13, 2023. https://www.who.int/news-room/fact-sheets/detail/infertility

17. Chandra A, Stephen EH. Infertility Service Use in the United States: Data From the National Survey of Family Growth, 1982–2010. 2014;(73):21.

18. American Society for Reproductive Medicine White Paper: Access to Care Summit.

19. ASRM Task Force on Diversity, Equity and Inclusion Issues Statement, Recommendations. Accessed July 14, 2022. https://www.asrm.org/about-us/initiatives/diversity-task-force/dei/asrm-task-force-on-diversity-equity-and-inclusion-issues-statement-recommendations/

20. 2020-25 Strategic Plan: Goals and Strategies. Accessed July 14, 2022. https://www.asrm.org/about-us/initiatives/Strategic-Plan/

Index

© The Editor(s) (if applicable) and The Author(s), under exclusive license to
Springer Nature Switzerland AG 2023
L. P. King, I. C. Band (eds.), *Case Studies in the Ethics of Assisted Reproduction*, https://doi.org/10.1007/978-3-031-41215-8

The manufacturer's authorised representative in the EU is Springer
Nature Customer Service Centre GmbH, Europaplatz 3, 69115 Heidelberg,
Germany. If you have any concerns regarding our products, please
contact ProductSafety@springernature.com

Printed and bound by CPI Group (UK) Ltd, Croydon, CR0 4YY

28/04/2026

02098202-0001